W9-DHU-377

HELEN M. STEVENS'
EMBROIDERED BIRDS

David & Charles

Title page: PLATE 1
Firecrest (Regulus ignicapillus) *and*
Norway spruce.
10.25 x 9cm (4 x 3½in)

This page: PLATE 2
Goldcrest (Regulus regulus) *and yew.*
10.25 x 9cm (4 x 3½in)

Contents page: PLATE 3
Rockhopper penguin (Eudyptes crstatus).
11.5 x 10.25cm (4½ x 4in)

In memory of Pookie

A DAVID & CHARLES BOOK

First published in 2003

Printed in

First published in the UK in 2003 by David & Charles Publishers,
Brunel House, Newton Abbot, Devon
ISBN 07153 1311 8

First published in the United States of America in 2003 by F & W Publishing,
4700 East Galbraith, Cincinnati 45236, OH 45236
1-800-289-0963

A catalogue record for this book is available from the British Library.

Photography by Nigel Salmon
Page layout by Nigel Morgan

Contents

HELEN M.
STEVENS

INTRODUCTION

HISTORY

In medieval England, when clerks documented for posterity the sumptuous gifts of embroidery donated to abbeys and monasteries by wealthy patrons, they coined a phrase *opus plumarium* – literally 'a work of feathers'. It described a form of embroidery that had evolved over the centuries, its origins perhaps long lost in Anglo-Saxon split stitch, which covered large fields of fabric in fluid, ever-changing sweeps of colour. Its name described its qualities perfectly; for just as the feathers on a bird's body change direction with the contours of the living creature beneath, so the arcing stitches of the technique create an illusion of three-dimensional life and movement.

Over twenty years ago, when I adopted *opus plumarium* as my 'signature' technique, I could only begin to guess at the scope and diversity of the subjects which I would illustrate through its versatility. Natural history subjects, of course: flora and fauna, foliate designs and underwater subjects; but also swathes of drapery, elements of the human form, machinery from steam engines to tractors, and stylised designs from illuminated initials to mythological beasts were all to be included. Not surprisingly, however, the subjects that best utilise its qualities are – birds!

Throughout the history of embroidery birds appear to be second only in popularity to elementary floral and geometric designs. From ancient Egypt to China, Scandinavia to the Americas, medieval to nineteenth century Europe and the modern world, they have always been the perfect subject for enthusiastic embroiderers. Whether worked in the stylised techniques of the ancients, the naïve vigour of the Middle Ages, the delicate tent stitch and blackwork of the Elizabethan period or the riotous Jacobean crewel and stump work, birds have brought beauty and inspiration to generations of stitchers. Virtually nothing has survived of the rich embroideries that so impressed the monastic inventory collators of medieval England (embroidery is an ephemeral art at best, and those pieces that were extant at the close of the Middle Ages almost certainly came to grief during the Reformation) but clues survive as to their content.

If we look to the illuminated manuscripts of England and Europe – a sister art form to fine embroidery – we glimpse the world of birds as the medievalists saw it. Many birds familiar to us today throughout the Northern hemisphere were clearly just as well recognised then; among them the elegant merlin, chattering swallow and magpie were all popular subjects, as were the omni-present pigeon and mallard duck (see Masterclass One, page 16). Mythical and legendary birds were also a feature of Saxon and later medieval art – the phoenix and roc were pan-cultural. Whatever else were the subjects of the long lost *opus plumarium* embroideries, it seems safe to assume that birds played an important role. Today, there is still a vast choice of embroidery techniques to enjoy but *opus plumarium* treated as a contemporary medium is still a magically evocative one.

◀ *PLATE 4*

The waxwing's (Bombycilla garrulus) *name is a direct link with the past – the bright red 'blobs' (actually tiny feathers) at the tip of some of its secondary flight feathers look like drops of molten wax, once used to seal letters and legal documents. Breeding in the Arctic and sub-Arctic, the waxwing is more common in continental Europe, though it occasionally arrives in very large numbers in Britain, often when there is a high yield of rowan berries, as the mountain ash is its favourite food source. These 'waxwing winters' are erratic and always worthy of note – one was recorded as early as the 1600s. Whether head or tail uppermost as a design feature, the contours of the birds are emphasised by the sweeping use of* opus plumarium.

Embroidery shown actual size

21.5 x 21.5cm (8½ x 8½in)

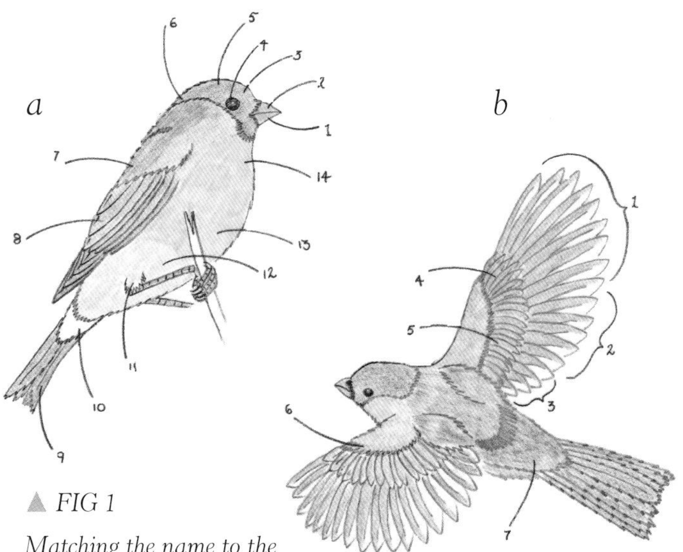

▲ *FIG 1*

Matching the name to the right part of the bird is essential to allow an easy understanding of descriptions and step-by-step guidance through the Masterclasses. Fig 1a and b show the anatomy of a 'typical' bird.

(a) At rest: 1 lower mandible; 2 upper mandible (1 and 2 together form the bill (beak) – seed eating); 3 forehead; 4 eye; 5 crown; 6 nape; 7 back; 8 wing; 9 tail; 10 undertail coverts; 11 leg feathers; 12 belly; 13 breast; 14 throat.

(b) In flight (seen from above): 1 primaries; 2 secondaries; 3 tertials (1, 2 and 3 together form the flight feathers); 4 primary coverts; 5 secondary coverts; 6 alula and upper wing; 7 rump.

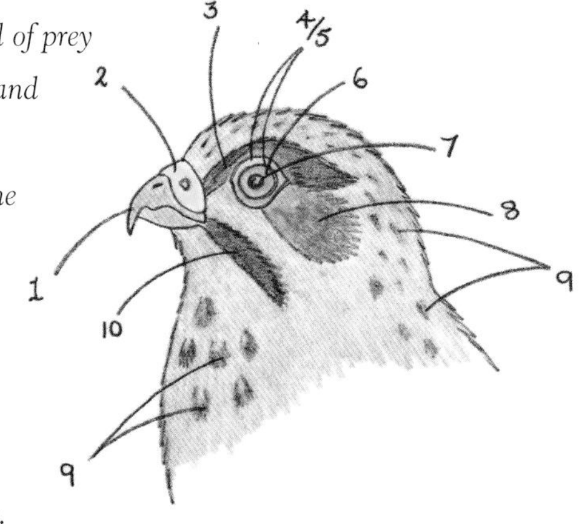

FIG 2 ▶

This 'composite' sketch of a bird of prey shows a number of the features and markings found on larger (and occasionally smaller species). The cere (2) is exclusive to raptors.

1 Bill (beak) – flesh eating; 2 cere; 3 supercilium; 4/5 orbital/eye ring; 6 coloured iris; 7 pupil; 8 ear coverts; 9 feather markings; 10 moustachial stripe.

Anatomy and Interpretation

Readers who come fresh to the Masterclass series will, in this book, be introduced to the basic uses of *opus plumarium* and its attendant techniques, the early chapters and the Stitch Variations section leading them stage by stage through the work. Those who have enjoyed the two previous titles in this series, *Helen M. Stevens' Embroidered Flowers* and *Embroidered Butterflies* will, I hope, find that the first chapters consolidate what they have already learned, whilst the later projects push out the boundaries of their confidence still further.

To work successful bird embroideries, however, we must do more than slavishly follow a template and colour chart. It is helpful to understand a little of the anatomy of our subjects – why the feathers flow as they do, how crests are raised in aggression or tails flared in courtship. Only then can we begin to appreciate why certain features and feathers should be emphasised, outlined or delineated by voiding and, eventually, design our own studies from scratch. Similarly, knowledge of birds' habitats, lifestyles and geographical range can ultimately help piece together a more complex picture. All these aspects of research and design are discussed as the book progresses.

Fig 1 (a and b) shows the basic anatomy of a 'typical' bird. Whereas not all birds share a similar spectrum of markings (eye ring, moustachial stripe and so on), the physiology that allows flight is virtually universal to all species: groupings of feathers into primary, secondary and tertial, for instance. Similarly, all birds sport a bill comprising an upper and lower mandible, though there are extraordinary differences between species, depending upon feeding techniques. Some of these characteristics are explained in Fig 2. Identification of markings and body parts necessary to appreciate descriptions and follow the charts is made easier by an understanding of these most commonly described features.

Working the Masterclasses

Each Masterclass introduces you to a specific aspect of bird embroidery and as the book progresses these become integrated, allowing you a greater scope of techniques within a single picture. Each subject is shown in an appropriate setting, the template and colour chart providing all you need to allow a step-by-step interpretation of the project. Full descriptions and working methods of the stitches required are given in Stitch Variations (page 92) and advice on threads, fabric and so on, under Materials (page 88) with additional suggestions throughout. Under Basic Techniques (page 90) you will find all you need to know about transferring your design and mounting your finished work.

Whilst the Masterclasses provide an opportunity to take entire projects from inception to completion exactly as illustrated, they also allow scope for personal interpretation. You can make choices as to background colour and the juxtaposition of additional features (insects, plants, water and so on), thus allowing you to create an entirely individual piece. Suggestions and advice as to these 'innovations' accompany each project. The colour plates and line drawings throughout each chapter are also explored in detail: elements of these studies may occasionally be incorporated into the Masterclass projects, or altered and recreated via your own interpretation. The more confident you become in your stitching the more tempted you may be to try your own sketching – there are a few hints on this, too!

When I began writing, sharing my thoughts, techniques and interpretations of nature in *The Embroiderer's Countryside,* I began to understand that simply observing nature was not quite enough for an embroiderer. The intimacies of our art are such that we need to enter into the world we aim to recreate. Because of the very character of our chosen medium, it invites the closest scrutiny, and that in turn means that we must invest every aspect of our work with spontaneity of detail that many other art forms do not – indeed cannot! The wicked glint reflected in both eye and beak of an eagle; the soft, downy pre-flight feathers of a near-fledgling chick; the iridescent sheen shared by common starling and exotic humming-bird; even the about-to-be-silenced buzz of a gnat as it darts past a flycatcher – embroidery can capture a moment in time and space and hold it fast to the fabric by the magic of thread.

I hope the images and information in this book will allow your imagination to soar with the eagle!

▲ *PLATE 5*

The kingfisher (Alcedo atthis) *was once known as the Halcyon bird, as it is chiefly seen during the hot, halcyon days of summer – though rarely even then, for few birds are shyer. All most of us can hope to see is a bright flash of lightning-blue plumage and a splash of water as a fish is caught. Wings outstretched, ready to dive, the underside of the wings can be seen here, the primary, secondary and tertial feathers evident from below (see Fig 1). Even the merest suggestion of a setting gives the main subject the benefit of a framework. This study is double mounted to give greater depth to the overall effect.*

6.5 x 10.35cm (2½ x 4in) (dimensions of inner mount)

HELEN M.
STEVENS

CHAPTER ONE

Friends and Neighbours

Like a pinprick in the azure gauze of the sky, the lark rises carolling its song whilst below, in the velvet darkness of a spinney, a wren scurries through the debris of the woodland floor. In the dappled tabby-weave of the hedgerow finches search for seeds and grain.

Man has always envied the ability to be 'as free as a bird' and whilst our most ancient ancestors were quick to discover their value as a source of food (Plate 6 and Fig 3), it cannot have been long before the decorative and entertainment qualities of birds were also appreciated. Exactly *when* birds first became domesticated is lost in time, but certainly when caves were our shelters, swallows also nested within their protective walls, and as huts and houses followed, so did the swallows' mud-pie nests, the birds' companionable chatter becoming Northern Europe's unmistakable sound of summer (Fig 4).

Today, domestic birds can be a fine source of inspiration and information, easily accessible to the artist and embroiderer. Get too close to a wild bird and it is likely to take flight – farmyard fowl, show birds and pets are far more likely to allow study of their plumage and 'jizz' (the characteristic stance and movement of a species which often makes distant identification possible when close-up inspection is not). Many familiar tame birds have counterparts in the countryside and an understanding of their anatomy and lifestyles is a useful introduction to the wider, wilder world of birds.

The term '*opus plumarium*' ('work of feathers') was coined in the early Middle Ages to describe the type of background-covering silk embroidery which is able to change direction smoothly to fill any field or contour without breaking ranks in the stitching – just

◄ *PLATE 6*

The 'Old English Pheasant' is actually a native of Asia, from the Caucasus to China. The earliest introductions were from the west of this range and sported no white neck ring. Later imports, from the eighteenth century, came from further east and bore the handsome white collar. As a result, we can tell the antecedents of all today's adult male pheasants. Chicks leave the nest within hours of hatching and begin to forage for themselves.

This study incorporates many essential techniques. On the large feathers we can see the structure of 'vaned' plumes – the barring and spotting as important on close-up work as on the portraits. The smaller, detailed feather incorporates directional opus plumarium *and floating embroidery which perfectly capture the qualities of downy feathering.*

Embroidery shown actual size

23 x 21.25cm (9 x 8½in)

FIG 3 ▶
Domestic fowl are a type of pheasant. They all derive from a single ancestor, the wild jungle fowl (Gallus gallus) *of Asia, probably first tamed during the Bronze Age around 4000*BC. *Long-vaned feathers, soft willowy plumage and differing textures, such as on the bird's comb and wattle, will all be discussed later.*

▲ *FIG 4*
The swallow's (Hirundo rustica) *nest is a dish of mud, strengthened by straw and grass and wedged against a beam or other support. Unlike pheasants and many domesticated breeds, the hungry chicks demand constant attention from their parents for around three weeks before they become independent.*

as the feathers on a bird's body are able to move with the bird (see Introduction). Into and around this basic silk work we can incorporate other techniques – to suggest markings within the plumage, voids to break between one plane and the next, high and low lights to create depth and perspective, but the main body of the design remains clothed with 'feather work'. A close look at familiar plumage will help to understand this technique.

Plate 6 shows a magnificent cock pheasant (*Phasianus colchicus*), his mate and their chicks, the main subject balanced by an elegant arc of close-up tail and body feathers. There is no firm evidence to support folklore that the pheasant was introduced into England by the Romans, but certainly it was established in the British Isles before the Norman conquest and is recorded in 1059. There are pheasant-like birds in the Bayeux Tapestry (late eleventh century) and they begin to appear in great detail in the illuminated manuscripts of the thirteenth and fourteenth centuries. They illustrate perfectly some of the many techniques we shall be exploring in this book.

The head and neck of the male pheasant (left Plate 6) is a symphony of rich, juxtaposed colours, each shade distinct from its neighbour, but with stitching smoothly merged. As the throat gives way to breast and belly, colours become more indistinct and flow into the next less abruptly whilst on the back large, patterned feathers are separated by fine voiding. As rump gives way to tail, soft shading is replaced by distinct bars of colour – softened by fine overlaid stitching. On the female, successive ranks of *opus*

◀ *PLATE 7*

*Peach-faced love-birds (*Agapornis roseicollis*) are popular aviary pets, deriving the name of love-bird from their habit of perpetual mutual preening. In the wild they prefer the dry, open habitats of the African continent, but have been bred for many years in captivity. The same shade of green silk has been used for back, neck and head – directional stitching alone is responsible for the apparent change in shade. Matching subject with setting is always a challenge – here a South African cape chestnut flower and buds fit the bill perfectly. Floating embroidery tipped with seed stitching suggests the delicate centre of the bloom.*
10 x 11.5cm (4 x 4½in)

▲*FIG 5*

Down feathers and semi-plumes (top and second top) are ideally described by a central shaft in stem stitch and barbs in floating embroidery. Vaned feathers (bottom) and those with a semi-plume type 'after feather' (second bottom) are achieved with a similarly worked central shaft and barbs in directional opus plumarium.

plumarium are scattered with Dalmatian dog spots (Stitch Variations, page 94), whilst the chicks are worked impressionistically, markings suggested by overlaid ticking (page 94).

The successful working of *opus plumarium* is dependent, above all else, on the correct alignment of the stitches. Both radial and directional *opus plumarium* (described in detail on pages 92–93) are essential elements in bird embroidery, but unlike simpler subjects such as flowers and butterflies (see the earlier titles in the Masterclass series), the 'core' toward which stitches must fall is not always easy to identify. Your subject may, of course, be shown from any number of perspectives, from full frontal to semi or full profile. Usually there is a combination of several angles: as in the male pheasant and the love bird (Plate 7, page 11), the back of the bird gives way to a swivelled neck and head in profile. The female pheasant presents a partly profiled head with a body to the front and an angled tail. How then can we always be sure that our stitches will fall convincingly?

The core or 'growing point' on a flower is its centre (usually the area of the pollen-bearing mass); similarly, on a butterfly it is the insect's body. On a centrally veined leaf the core is elongated – the ridge down its middle forms the backbone of the stitches, towards which they must fall. On a bird, the core of the stitching is the tip of the subject's beak, on individual feathers it is the long shaft which runs through its middle (Fig 5). The *opus plumarium* is worked, respectively, as either radial (converging to a central point) or directional (falling back toward an elongated core). Identifying the angle of stitching towards the shaft of a single feather is relatively simple but maintaining a radial flow can be more tricky, especially when planes of perspective break the flow, as in the case of the hen pheasant's head and body. The key to working this type of subject successfully is to think three-dimensionally. Where the more distant elements of the subject disappear behind the closer, imagine the line of continuity. Picture the flow of the stitches as they fall towards the core, and, as the contour reappears simply follow through.

As well as technique, successful embroidery also depends upon design. The best bird identification handbooks show their subjects in appropriate settings and from a variety of perspectives – those dull 'mugshots' of birds once so common have now largely given way to much more inspirational illustrations. We should also give a little thought to our subject's surroundings and although a little artistic license is certainly allowed, we should try to avoid obvious inconsistencies. The pheasant family is in a simple grassy environment; the love bird, though more often seen in captivity as an aviary bird, is shown with a flower spray appropriate to its native habitat; in Plate 8 here, a goldfinch (*Carduelis carduelis*) is shown with a favourite food source, a dry teasel-head.

◀ *PLATE 8*
The goldfinch is one of the easiest birds to encourage into your garden (see Chapter Three), and once intent upon feeding can become quite oblivious to spectators. Like all finches it has a strong beak designed to pry out and crack seeds. Here, the bird is seen almost full-faced – the head turned only slightly to one side. Radial opus plumarium *falls back toward the core (beak tip), smoothly arcing over the back of the head, a subdued void suggesting where throat gives way to breast. The bird's lower body is worked strata by strata, each blending into the next, or separated by more subdued voiding as appropriate.*
9.25 x 22.5cm (3¾ x 8¾in)

In the Middle Ages and right into the early part of the last century, goldfinches were often kept as captive songbirds. Today, in many countries, the thought of keeping wild birds in cramped, inhospitable cages is abhorrent (the practice is often illegal) and thankfully pet birds are restricted to those bred for the purpose, including parrots, budgies and canaries. Show birds such as Norwich canaries can be as spectacular as any wild finch and roller (song) canaries (Fig 6) just as delightfully vocal as the once popular caged linnet.

▲ *FIG 6*

Wild canaries still thrive in the Canary Islands whence they were exported as cage birds as early as the 1500s. Typical finches (see Plate 8), they are seed-eaters and fine songsters. Native stock is olive/green with variable streaking – the vibrant golds and yellows of domestic stocks are the product of selective breeding.

Truly tame domestic pets probably represent our best chance of watching and studying small birds at very close quarters.

Birds are the most brightly coloured of all vertebrates, and although vivid plumage is by no means universal (a general rule of thumb is the hotter the climate, the brighter the bird), it is a joy to be able to see these little jewels at close quarters. The different hues on bright plumage are built up in two ways – by pigment and structure. Pigments produced in the bird's body (often dependant upon its foodstuff) are responsible for browns, tans, yellows, oranges and many shades of red. Blues and most greens are due to feather structure. Barbs reflect blue or green light and filter the rest of the spectrum – white is produced by barbs which reflect almost all light. Iridescent effects, such as on the head and neck of the cock pheasant or mallard drake (*Anas platyrhynchos*) (Plate 10), are effected by a refinement of the same process.

The overall appearance of the plumage – whether richly mat or vibrantly shiny – depends upon how each feather lies. Feathers with their flat surfaces exposed usually create a shiny effect; stubby feathers at right angles to the body create a duller, velvet sheen. By watching the way plumage reacts to the bird's movement, the shine responding to the changing angle of light, we can appreciate just why '*opus plumarium*' was so named.

Even when the smooth contours of *opus plumarium* are shattered by adapting the technique to create a contrasting effect (as on the body of the chick to the left in Plate 9) the direction of the individual stitches is all important to the successful description of the subject. The duckling (right) is worked in radial *opus plumarium,* stitches falling smoothly back to the 'bean' at the tip of the bill. On the chick, a fluffy effect is created by working short, straight, separate stitches – but keeping the overall flow converging on the growing point at the beak. These stubby stitches are softened by overlaying slightly longer stitches in a finer thread, subduing the voids and creating a powder-puff effect at the outer edge while maintaining the directional sweep.

Masterclass One (Plate 10) features a handsome mallard drake dabbling in the water, and considering a wayward snail as an appetiser to lunch! In this study we will be concentrating mainly on the principles of radial *opus plumarium* worked in broad swathes of colour – individual strata merging smoothly, whether from shade to self-shade or from contrasting colour to colour. Other simple techniques have been incorporated to shadow, soften and in places highlight the subject (you can recap these techniques in Stitch Variations before you begin the project). The setting, whilst offering entertainment value, has been kept simple to allow the eye to concentrate on the complex patterning of the duck's plumage. Follow the steps sequentially through the project and using relatively few techniques you can recreate this familiar yet spectacular resident of the local village pond.

◀ *PLATE 9*

A fluffy pair – chick and duckling – snuggle together for warmth. Despite their different lifestyles, they share much in common as youngsters: like the pheasant chicks they leave the nest quickly and are able to seek food independently, though the principle of safety in numbers tends to make broods stick together. The chick's beak is well adapted to foraging for grain and small insects, whilst the duckling already dabbles in the water for food. At the end of his beak is a sharp 'bean' used to break free of the tough eggshell which remains into adult life (see Masterclass One, Plate 10).

9 x 9.5cm (3½ x 3¾in)

MALLARD DRAKE

The handsome mallard is a welcome sight on any waterway. Bottle green head feathers are separated from slightly more sober body plumage by a bright white collar. Striking wing bars – white, black and teal – are complemented by the jaunty flip of upturned tail feathers. Simple arcing fronds of water plants and a questing snail complete the design.

The embroidery is shown on a pale background (see Materials page 88). Referring to Basic Techniques (page 90) transfer the design from the template on page 18 on to the fabric, making sure all details are included, and then mount the transferred pattern into a tambour hoop. Keep the fabric as taut as possible within the hoop to make stitching easier.

TECHNIQUES

This striking study is achieved with only six basic stitches:

Stem stitch • Radial *opus plumarium*
Directional *opus plumarium* • Ticking • Snake stitch
Straight stitch

This study concentrates on using broad swathes of *opus plumarium*. You may find it helpful to complete the whole of the shadow lining on the duck before you begin these filling stitches. On a large subject such as this it is useful to build up a rhythm whilst stitching broad fields of colour which you will not want to break by reverting to linear techniques.

PLATE 10 ▶

Masterclass One: Embroidery shown actual size 25 x 18.5cm (9¾ x 7¼in)

HELEN M.
STEVENS

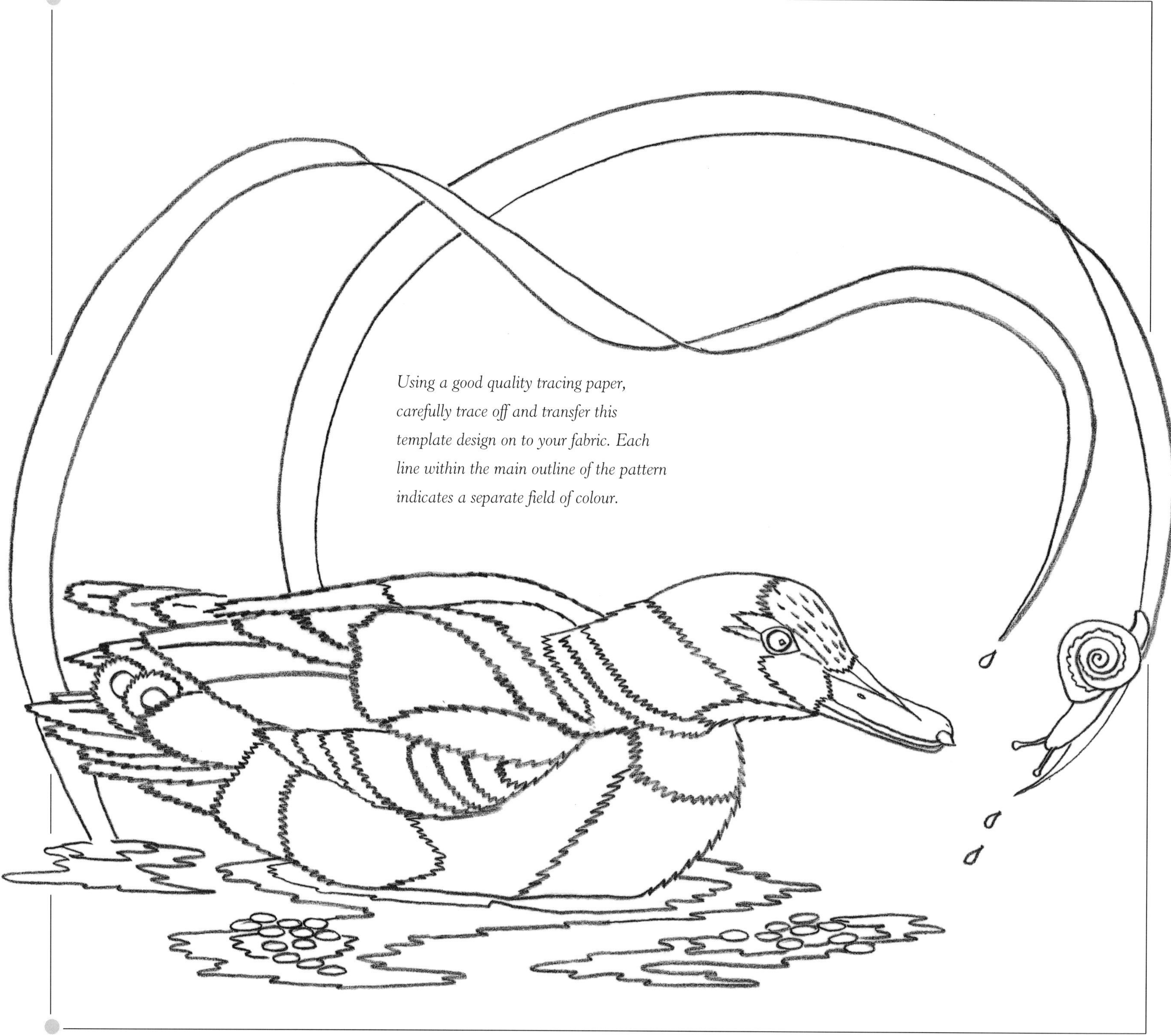

Using a good quality tracing paper, carefully trace off and transfer this template design on to your fabric. Each line within the main outline of the pattern indicates a separate field of colour.

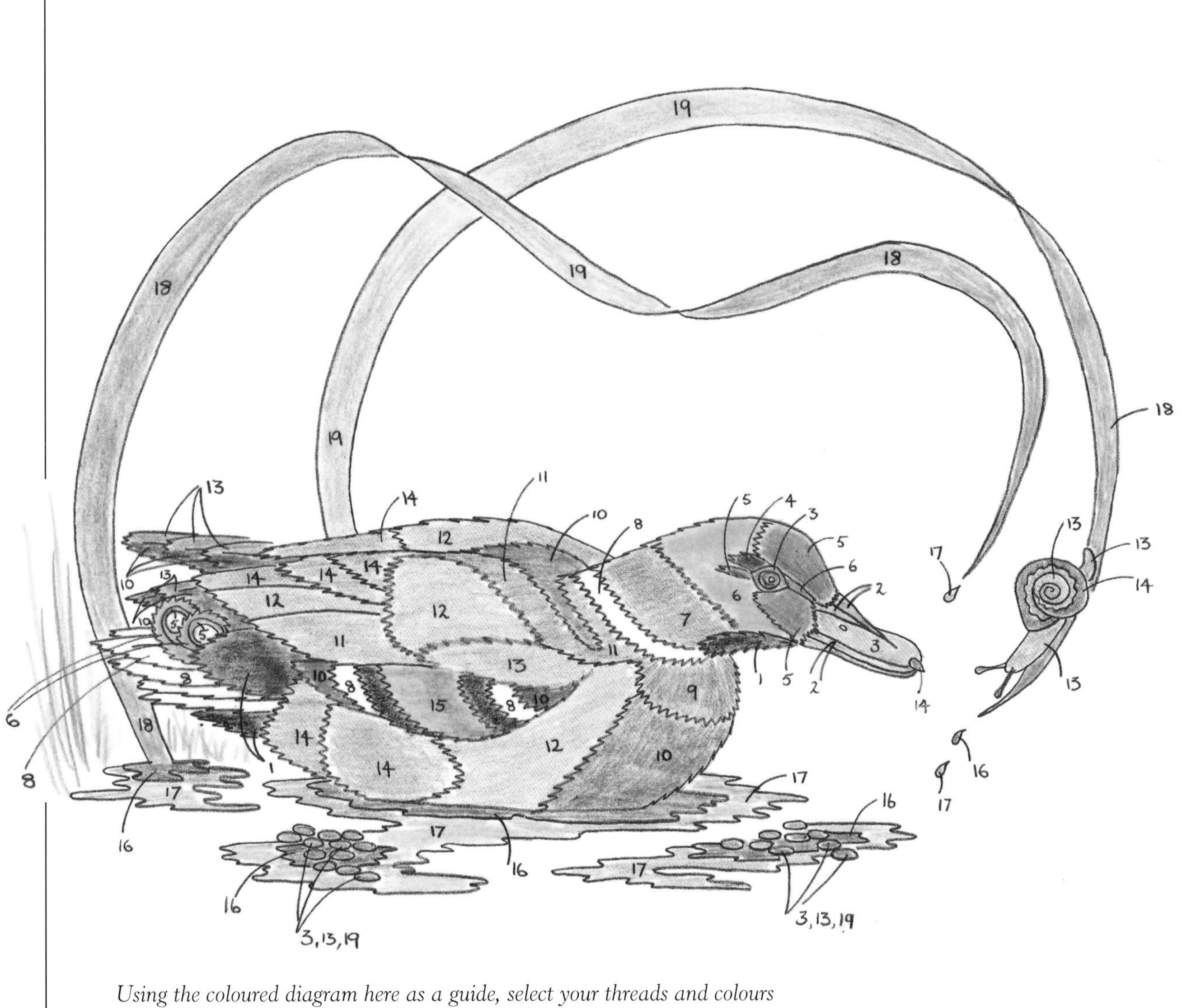

Using the coloured diagram here as a guide, select your threads and colours according to the advice given in the Introduction and Materials section. Remember that the colours shown here are not intended to be representative of the actual shades (refer to Plate 10 to choose these accurately – the names suggested in the list should help with this) but are designed to assist in the charting process. Where several areas of the same colour abut, such as the white tail feathers, these are not always annotated separately, in order to simplify the chart.

Suggested Colours

1 Black
2 Yellow
3 Deep yellow
4 Deep purple
5 Dark bottle green
6 Medium bottle green
7 Light bottle green
8 White
9 Dull mauve
10 Deep brown
11 Lilac grey
12 Ecru
13 Beige
14 Light grey
15 Teal
16 Green-blue
17 Light blue
18 Dark green
19 Yellow-green

Design Notes

The imagined light source in this study comes from a point immediately above the main subject.

Begin with the Mallard...

Referring to Plate 10, work the smooth and fragmented shadow lining in fine black (1) thread on the underside of each main feature of the duck.

1 In yellow (2) and deep yellow (3) respectively work the sections of the upper bill in radial *opus plumarium* converging very loosely upon the 'bean' at the tip. Fill the narrow fields forming the lower bill with broad stem stitch in yellow. Work the bean in a few straight stitches in light grey (14). Infill the eye with black straight stitching and surround it with a line of fine stem stitch in deep yellow and a similar fine line in black. Highlight the eye with a single white (8) seed stitch. Beginning with the fields closest to the bill, work radial *opus plumarium* in receding strata of dark bottle green (5), medium bottle green (6) and light bottle green (7) and the small eye patch of deep purple (4). Work the throat area similarly in black. Highlight the upper head with ticking stitches in light bottle green.

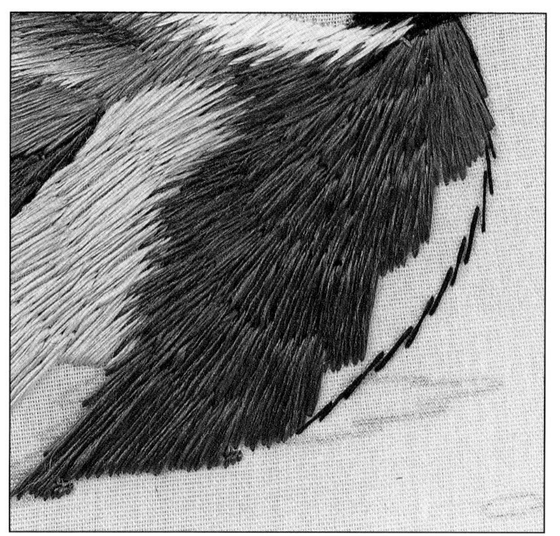

2 When the head and upper neck is complete, work the white collar and then move down to the breast. Carefully angling your stitches toward the throat, work strata of dull mauve (9) and deep brown (10). As the *opus plumarium* meets and abuts the shadow line, merge the stitches smoothly. Begin to work strata of ecru (12) along the main lower body.

3 With a similarly smooth merging of colours, work the lilac grey (11), deep brown, ecru and beige (13) strata of the back and the first of the large lower back feathers. Void or blend with the shadow lines as appropriate between the ecru and light grey (14) strata, and merge the beige strata into the fragmented shadow line above the wing. Refer to Plate 10 to ensure that you are following the correct directional sweep.

4 Work the bold wing stripes in successive strata (beginning with those closest to the head) of deep brown, white, black, teal (15), black, white and deep brown respectively. If you have a slightly darker shade of teal, intersperse a few stitches of this darker shade to give added depth to this stratum. Returning to the breast and belly, continue smooth strata of ecru and light grey, blending or voiding between strata as appropriate.

5 Continue as above to describe the lower back and rump. The tips of the folded wings and the tail feathers are worked in directional *opus plumarium*, the angle slanting very obliquely toward straight stitched shafts central to each large feather. Central shafts should be worked in light grey, then from the top work wing tips in beige and deep brown and the tail feathers in white. Work the curly 'duck's tail' feathers in two strata of snake stitch in deep and medium bottle green. Complete the duck by working fine straight stitches to subdue the voids and soften the contours of the shadow lining, referring to Plate 10.

Moving on to the Surrounding Features...

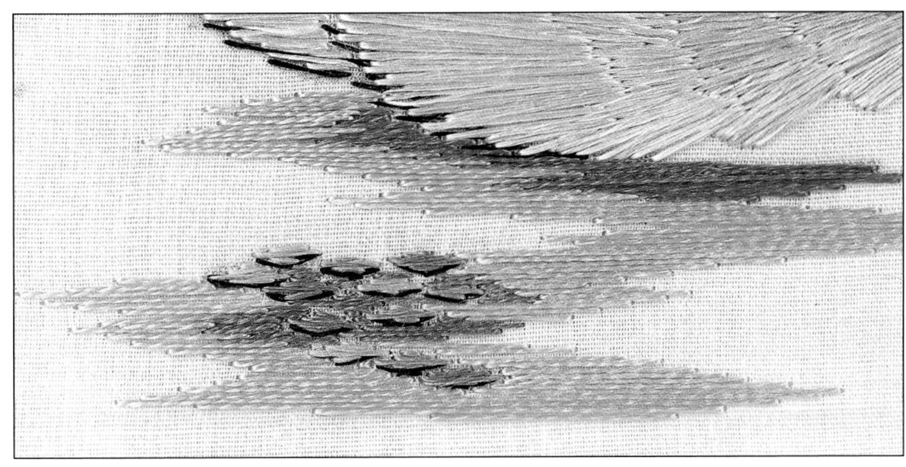

6 Shadow line the underside of each floating segment of duck-weed and work randomly in yellow, beige or yellow-green (19), filling each with a few short, straight horizontal stitches. If you have it, use lightly twisted or plied cotton or silk for the water, for a rippling effect. Fill the appropriate fields in long straight horizontal stitching in green-blue (16) and light blue (17).

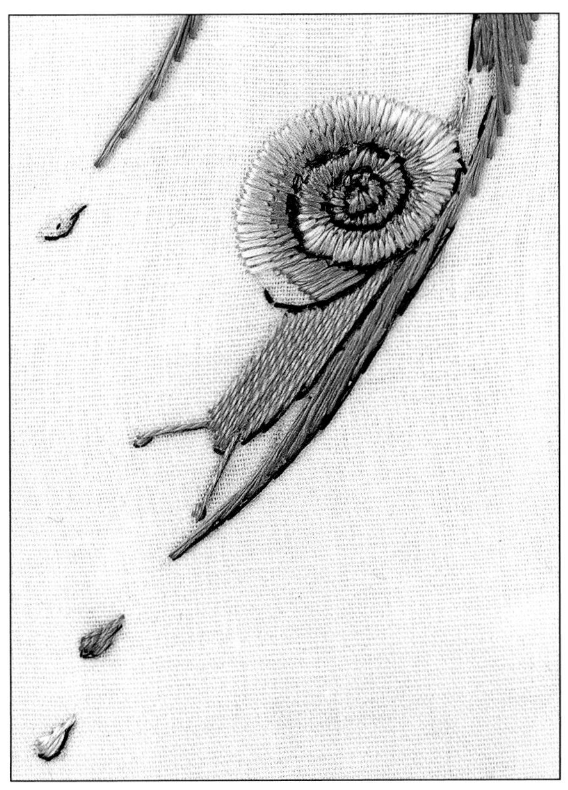

7 The tiny water droplets should each be shadow lined (top) and infilled in diagonal straight stitching in green and light blue as shown. Shadow line the snail and work his body in very loosely angled snake stitching in beige (again, if you have a choice of textures, use a mat thread). Work the shell in two strata of tightly angled snake stitching in beige and light grey.

Finally, referring to Plate 10, work the aquatic plant leaves in broad swathes of snake stitch in dark green (18) and yellow-green. Suggest reeds and grasses by working long straight stitches in dark green and yellow-green (using a change of texture of you have it) angled toward the base of the plant.

HELEN M.
STEVENS

CHAPTER TWO

Birds of Prey

Between a green and gold patchwork of meadows and fields, silver-grey ribbons of roads and motorways interlace the countryside. Far above, eyes ever watchful for the least scurrying movement in the wayside grasses, the kestrel hovers, motionless but for a quiver in its outstretched wings.

The kestrel (*Falco tinnunculus*) (Plate 11) is one of the late twentieth century's success stories. Whilst falling prey to the use of pesticides on arable land some decades ago, the growth of the motorway system with its attendant vast acreage of wide grass verges has provided an unexpected, and tailor-made, habitat. Traffic islands and the like, untouched by chemicals, allow small mammals and large insects to thrive – and the kestrel's larder to expand accordingly. One of the few joys of motorway travel is to witness the kestrel's motionless flight, wings spread to catch the breeze, the long stillness followed by a lightning-fast 'stoop' as the bird plummets to earth, talons extended, to make its kill.

The old country names of 'wind-hover' and 'stand-gale' explain the falcon's technique: the bird heads into the wind and stands still by flying at precisely the prevailing wind speed. By adjusting the angle of wings and tail it is able to match the airflow perfectly, whether in calm or gusty conditions. Those outstretched feathers are a perfect subject through which to explore the dynamics of embroidering the open wings of a bird in flight.

As already discussed, the principles of *opus plumarium* decree that all our stitches must converge upon the core, or growing point, of the subject – in most cases the tip of the beak. However, there are occasions when a major feature, such as an extended wing, needs to pivot around a secondary core, a fulcrum which, when the wing is folded, would

◀ *PLATE 11*

The early morning sun burns through hazy clouds to aid the kestrel in its first foray of the day. Its hovering technique, head into the wind, suggests that on completely calm days it would be unable to hunt, but at high altitudes the air is never entirely still and so it is able to use thermals and other eddies to maintain its flight.

The pure silk of the bird is contrasted by using a mat cotton thread for the landscape below, in turn complemented by a still-different texture to the sky. The sun is worked in a single strand of pure silk, clouds similarly and a shimmering effect created by the use of a cellophane thread, matching the horizontal stitching perfectly, overlaid to blur the outline between sun and sky.

Embroidery shown actual size
20.25 x 20.25cm (8 x 8in)

▲ *FIG 7*

A quick sketch comparing the peregrine falcon (left) and the goshawk illustrates the differing wing outline (see text). Using pastel crayons it is easy to suggest wing barring by simply using one colour on top of another. In a miniature embroidery try laddering – work the underlying strata first and then needleweave through the stitches with a contrasting colour following the contour of the bar.

allow the feathers to merge with the main flow of the body but which, when the wing is open, allows the stitches to flow toward itself. In a study such as Plate 11, the stitching on the beak, head, throat and breast all flows back to the core; similarly the Dalmatian dog work on the back flows and 'disappears' as if to converge with the other stitches. The wings, however, both far and near side, appear to converge slightly differently – they each fall to a secondary core at the bird's shoulders.

To complete this sequence of working successfully, follow the usual principles of working toward the core (in this case secondary) and build up the strata of stitches sequentially: first the upper wing, then the coverts and finally the flight feathers, primaries, secondaries and tertials. (Refer to Fig 1, page 6 for a reminder of anatomy.) Barring and other markings can be added later in shooting stitches or ticking as appropriate.

The female kestrel's chestnut brown, black-barred tail tipped with white differentiates her from the male – his lower back and tail are the same silver grey as his head. The long tail feathers, so essential to the motionless hover that allows successful hunting, should be worked individually, the central shaft of each feather forming an elongated core for acutely angled fields of directional *opus plumarium*: here, chestnut, black and white respectively, barred in black shooting stitch.

Small birds of prey fall into two distinct categories: falcons and hawks. Their outline in flight allows identification – colours often appear similar when silhouetted against a bright, sunlit sky (Fig 7). Wing shape is the key and is linked to the habitats in which the birds live and hunt. Falcons (such as the kestrel) are birds of open country with wings built for speed – long with acutely angled tips. Hawks on the other hand are birds of woodland or countryside with scattered shrubs and copses. Their wings are shorter, broader and more suited to quick manoeuvres – wing tips are broadly triangular, the third or fourth primaries longer than the first.

The goshawk (*Accipiter gentilis*) (Plate 12) is an efficient hunter in scrubby, low-lying woodland areas, its strong, agile wings allow it to swoop down upon its prey silently, its

◀ *PLATE 12*

*Nature's food chain is an inescapable though sometimes distressing truth. Small birds such as the whitethroat (*Sylvia communis*) prey upon insects, and themselves often become victims of raptors. Left to its own devices, however, the balance of predator and prey usually finds a proper balance: only when man interferes is the equilibrium upset. The nest of the whitethroat is often found amid bright green early foliage and this, together with the pink and white hawthorn blossom, lifts a picture otherwise comprised of browns and greys. Fine detail, in the shape of the dancing gnats, is contrasted with the miniaturisation of the distant goshawks.*

13.5 x 22.25cm (5¼ x 8¾in)

▶ *PLATE 13*

Eagles have been symbols of power for thousands of years. Like the Romans, Napoleon, the Russian imperial court and many others before them, the United States of America has used the eagle's aura of majesty to convey its own authority. As 'King of the Birds' in folklore, the eagle also proclaims its own supremacy, although it is outwitted in a flying contest by the tiny wren (see Plate 19, page 45) who hides beneath its wing until the final moments of the race.

Here the portrait is double mounted to emphasise the importance of the subject. Stretched on a small inner board, it is then applied to a larger mount covered in gold slub silk complementing the colours of the embroidery. 9 x 9cm (3½ x 3½in) (inner mount)

almost owl-like approach delivering the *coup de grâce* with powerful claws. Its size (up to 60cm/24in) means that whilst smaller prey may be taken, larger targets are often preferred: pigeons, crows and game birds are favourites – the whitethroat may well escape its fate if a more substantial meal is on offer! The two distant birds in Plate 12 show typical flight postures: wings drawn back for the drop (top) and broad cruising attitude (right). It is possible to capture the essence of even a large bird on a small scale by paring irrelevant detail down to the bare minimum.

Miniaturisation – a useful device to create depth and distance in the simplest of pictures – requires the application of a few simple but important guidelines. To miniaturise a subject successfully we need to capture the 'essentials' whilst dispensing with less vital details. Here, the shape, colour and jizz of the birds are vital. Shadow lining is necessary to outline the subject against the 'sky' and definite indications of primary markings are all important. If possible, use a finer thread than your choice for close-up elements of the design and work the base colours, adhering to the principles of directional work, without interrupting the flow by use of Dalmatian dog or other decorative techniques. You can add markings later in ticking, small shooting or laddering stitches (see Fig 7). Tiny, almost subliminal touches, such as the eye highlights are still important to give the subject life. True miniaturisation is almost impressionistic – unlike the art of the miniature portrait (Plate 13).

The magnificent bald eagle (*Haliaeetus leucocephalus*), the national bird of the United States of America, is not, of course, bald but rather endowed with a head-dress of pure white feathers (see also Fig 15 page 58). This, together with its black supercilium and wicked yellow beak gives the bird its familiar aspect of stern authoritarianism. Here, although the overall size of the study is small, fine details and subtle nuances are vital to capture the full import of the subject. Shadow line carefully, including individual feathers, and blend grey into the white plumage below the beak and eye to further enhance the three-dimensional effect achieved by the shadowing. Radial *opus plumarium* over the head should be worked converging upon the beak, blending into directional *opus plumarium* describing the small feathers, each falling back to a central shaft. Soften the zone between the supercilium and the white plumage by feathering out fine shooting stitches to subdue the demarcation line.

The expression 'eagle eyed' is actually better suited to the kestrel than the eagle! Whilst the kestrel's stoop of over 30m (100ft) can be the result of spotting a half inch long beetle, the eagle's prey is invariably bigger – and consequently less difficult to spot. Waterfowl and marsh rabbits are often taken and even the young of large animals such as spotted deer are not safe. Bully-boy tactics are not unknown as the bald eagle is fond of fish and whilst occasionally catching its own is known to harass that expert angler the osprey, forcing it to drop its catch which is retrieved with spectacular aerobatics by the antagonist before it even hits the water.

Whilst the keen eyesight of day-flying raptors has become a byword for observation, so the night vision of their nocturnal counterparts is also legendary. Set to the front of their heads, owls' eyes (like our own) are designed for three-dimensional vision – most birds

▲ *FIG 8*

The eyes of the tawny owl face forward in contrast to those of the kestrel which are designed for more 'all round' vision. The size of the eye in both cases indicates the importance of good vision for hunting. Always work the eye in advance of the surrounding embroidery – it is easier to work around a feature than to leave a blank and fill it in later.

▲ *PLATE 14*

Young tawny owlets are wedged into a hollow branch to prevent their falling and are fed by their parents for about five weeks before fledging. Even then they are dependent upon their parents for another three months before they begin to fend for themselves.

Wool is surface couched loosely towards the base of the design to create the mossy effect, the bark of the tree worked in mat stranded cotton. Soften the voids between various planes of stitching by overlaying fine shooting stitches and emphasise the eyes with bright white highlights.
10.25 x 10.25cm (4 x 4in)

have eyes set to the side of their heads (see Fig 8). The huge retina of each eye is extremely sensitive to light, allowing vision in very poor conditions. The tawny owl (*Strix aluco*) also has exceptional hearing, with ears set asymmetrically (higher to the left and lower to the right side of the head) so no slight rustle of the night-time undergrowth goes unnoticed. These useful adjuncts to the tawny owl's hunting skills are essential, especially given that young owls are dependent upon their parents for food for over four months (Plate 14).

In some uncanny way the tawny owl seems able to assess the season's hunting before it begins. In years when prey will be scarce only one or two eggs are laid; when there is to be plentiful food a larger clutch is laid and hatched, each chick emerging at intervals of about two days. Early in life the chicks are covered with a mottled brown-grey down – a new challenge if we are to capture it in embroidery.

Owls are an almost unique subject in embroidery in that facially they present not a single core but a more complicated pattern of stitching. The 'facial disc' (which serves as a reflector, collecting sounds and focusing them on the ears) means that feathers, in our case, stitches, radiate around each eye, creating (as on the open wings of the kestrel) two secondary cores, converging upon the beak and then merging back into a single radial sweep are the outer face is reached. In the young owls this is less pronounced than on the adult as the texture of the down is uniform (Plate 15, Masterclass Two). Here is a perfect opportunity, if you are able to work in a fine thread, to blend several colours together in the needle to make a single, broader gauge comprised of various shades. Build up your strata roughly to emphasise the irregularity of the down giving way to immature feathers, and soften the whole by overlaying shooting stitches in increasingly fine strands, finally allowing these to stand proud of the last strata of main stitching.

The tawny owl is Britain's most common owl, its territory also extending through parts of Europe into the Far East, a range largely shared with the little owl (Fig 9). The range of the barn owl (*Tyto alba*) is, however, much broader. Throughout the United States, South America, much of Africa, the Middle East and India, Indonesia and Australia, the barn owl's silent flight and startling, prolonged shriek are familiar night-time phenomenon. In Europe during the Middle Ages it was considered by townsfolk to be a bird of ill omen – Chaucer referred to it as the 'prophet of woe and mischance' – but farmers always knew it as a friend and many medieval and later barns boast purpose-built 'owl windows' high in the apex of roofs to allow 'Old Hushwing' access, for as a hunter of vermin the barn owl is unsurpassed.

A family of two adults rearing their young owlets may take up to a thousand rodents during a three-month nesting period – a serious help to farmers – as well as a variety of other prey. Sparrows and starlings may also be taken and in some areas grass snakes (Fig 10), frogs and other amphibians make up a significant part of the diet. Most owls will also take advantage of large, tasty moths or beetles that ill-advisedly venture into the open during the bird's hunting foray.

In Masterclass Two we use the barn owl in flight to explore the use of radial *opus plumarium* falling back to secondary cores, both on the open wings and the face of the bird. A shimmering crescent moon and the dash to safety of a vibrant red underwing moth complete a study that is all movement.

▲ *FIG 9*

*The little owl's (*Athene noctua*) prey is more insect-oriented than most owls but also includes molluscs, worms and spiders. Here a 'harvestman' is about to fall prey. Don't be afraid to sketch roughly and add details later. White markings on this little fellow will be added at the embroidery stage – the spider will not be transferred but will be added freehand at the end of the project (see drawing on page 87 and Masterclass Five).*

◀ *FIG 10*

*The grass snake (*Natrix natrix*) is quite harmless to humans and may be distinguished from the poisonous adder by its green colouring – which may be light or dark. Snakes that do not fall prey to birds or other predators can live up to nine years. If you are fortunate enough to spot one it may be a willing model: a basking snake may lie motionless in the sun for hours.*

BARN OWL IN FLIGHT

Gold, silver and blue-grey silks are complemented by an occasional flash of silver metallic thread in this striking, slightly stylised study. The facial disc features two secondary cores to the stitching in the shape of the forward-facing eyes, highlighted to 'follow' the viewer. The frantic dash of the moth may just have escaped notice!

Shown here on a black background, the design could be transferred on to a pale fabric (see notes accompanying the template) but if so careful shadow lining would be needed on all features, including individual feathers. On both template and colour chart the facial markings are simplified as most of these are applied after the main stitching is complete – as is the barring and ticking on the rest of the bird.

You may find it helpful to refer to the Stitch Variations section to remind yourself of the various decorative stitches that overlay the groundwork. Complete each area of underlying embroidery before you begin to apply the decorative techniques and try to work symmetrically, building up each side of the study evenly, section by section.

TECHNIQUES

This study is a blend of basic linear, filling and decorative stitches:

Straight stitch • Stem stitch • Radial *opus plumarium*
Directional *opus plumarium* • Ticking
Shooting stitch • Seed stitch
Surface couching

PLATE 15 ▶

Masterclass Two: Embroidery shown life size 19.5 x 21cm (7¾ x 8¼in)

HELEN M.
STEVENS

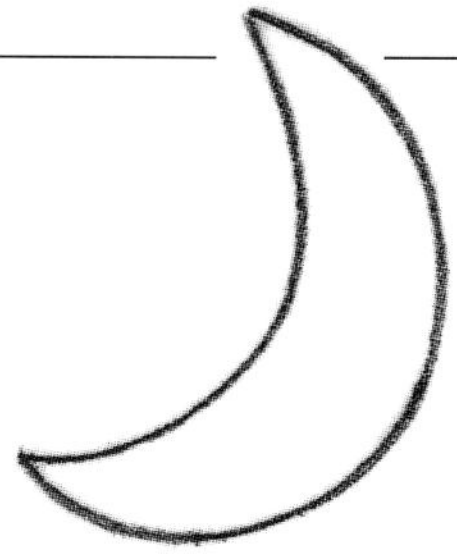

Whether working on pale or dark fabric, transfer the outline from the template carefully, checking that you have included all the details. If you choose to work on a pale ground, use a carbon paper of medium shade (orange or light blue) that will not be too hard to disguise with white and grey threads.

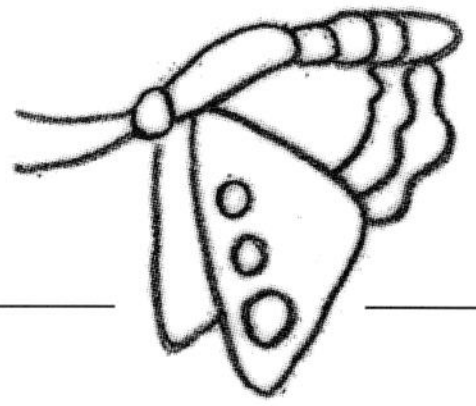

Suggested Colours

1 Black
2 Champagne yellow
3 White
4 Old gold
5 Gold
6 Silver
7 Grey
8 Dark blue-grey
9 Lilac grey
10 Red
11 Metallic silver

Choose your colours in a good light – preferably daylight – making sure each skein is clearly labelled. If you work later under different lighting conditions it is not always easy to distinguish between the various grey and silver shades. If you are able to use a very fine thread (see notes on threads in Materials), try mixing two or more strands of white, silver or grey in your needle to create a single shade: this is how the 'shot' effect is created in Plate 15. Where an area (such as number 8) is indicated by a black wavy line ᔑ this indicates that a decorative technique/colour is used similarly throughout that section of the design.

Design Notes

Working on a black background, the lack of a shadow line means that particular care must be taken with your directional stitching and voiding. Refer to Plate 15 to make sure that the flow of the opus plumarium *is correct. Vary the gauge of your thread as appropriate – use finer strands for softening strata and subduing voids.*

Begin With The Owl's Face . . .

Remember, there are two secondary cores to the work on the face of the owl.

1 Infill the eyes with straight stitching in black (1), work the eye ring in fine stem stitch in champagne yellow (2) and highlight in white seed stitches (3). Work the beak in Champagne yellow in a wedge of radial *opus plumarium*, dividing and lowlighting with two straight stitches in black. Converging upon each eye, work a stratum of radial *opus plumarium* in white, followed by a second stratum, blending with the first toward the outside of the head, and voiding toward the inside (right side of the face as shown).

Separate the strata and void around the beak. Work fine shooting stitches in white across the voids to soften the contours (shown on left side). Complete the outer face and two upper strata in old gold (4) and gold (5) respectively and subdue voids as appropriate.

2 Work the throat and breast in strata of silver (6) and white and overlay ticking in dark blue-grey (8).

Complete the owl's feet (voiding between each toe) in Champagne yellow straight stitching and overlay at right angles in straight stitches in black (right and left respectively as shown).

For the tail feathers, work a straight stitched central shaft in Champagne yellow, the outer side of each feather in white and the inner in silver in directional *opus plumarium*. Work the barred markings in shooting stitch in dark blue-grey. Complete the two small wedges under each wing in gold radial work, and soften all contours and voids with fine shooting stitches in the appropriate shades.

Building Up Each Wing Sequentially . . .

3 Work from the inside out, following the colour chart and Plate 15 for guidance. Work respective strata in radial *opus plumarium* in gold, white and silver, voiding and merging the strata as appropriate. Work the straight stitched shafts for the coverts in Champagne yellow and complete the feathers by working directional *opus plumarium*: inner strata in white, outer (at the tip of each feather) in dark blue-grey. Work the long central shaft of each flight feather in narrow stem stitch in Champagne yellow.

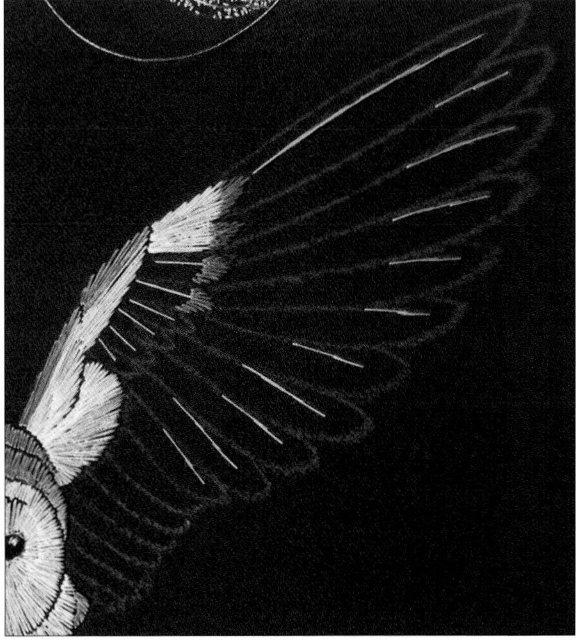

4 Work either side of each flight feather (primaries, secondaries and tertials) in directional *opus plumarium* in gold (topmost only), white, silver and grey (7) as appropriate and overlay the barring in shooting stitch in dark blue-grey.

Complete the smaller markings on the inner wing and coverts in ticking stitches in dark blue-grey. Soften strata and voids as necessary with shooting stitches in the appropriate shades, allowing these stitches to overlap the outline of the design on the lower tertials.

5 Review the whole of the motif and, as you feel appropriate, subdue voids and soften strata with fine shooting stitches. Remember subduing and so on, should be worked in the shade of the motif nearer to the viewer (see Stitch Variations, page 92). Allow these stitches to overlap the outer contours of the motif to create the effect of soft, downy feathers. Finally, referring to Plate 15, work shooting stitches in black to lowlight and outline the facial discs, and work two short straight stitches in metallic silver (11) on either side of the beak.

Moving On To The Moth And The Moon . . .

6 Work black Dalmatian dog spots on the upper wing and a band of black on the lower. Flood lilac grey (9) and red (10) *opus plumarium* respectively around these features. Working toward the head of the moth, work several voided strata of *opus plumarium* to create the segmented head and body of the insect. Referring to Plate 15, work straight stitches in metallic silver to describe the antennae and segmentation lines.

7 Infill the crescent moon with dotting stitches in lilac grey and metallic silver. Surface couch the outline of the moon in metallic silver.

HELEN M.
STEVENS

CHAPTER THREE

TOWN AND COUNTRY

However chic and fashionable a city courtyard or tranquil and beautiful a country garden may be, a vibrant backdrop of container-grown shrubs or flower-beds of colourful annuals are made all the more special by the birds that make a garden their home. They are the twinkling jewels that enhance the most inspired canvas.

Large or small, the birds that visit our gardens bestow upon us the privilege of allowing wildlife into our own domestic space – and there is a thrill in the knowledge that they stay of their own free will. Commercial producers of bird food enjoy a thriving trade in pandering to our desire for the presence of wild birds but there is much that we can do to encourage such guests without resorting to a great deal of expense. Sunflowers, Michaelmas daisies and ornamental thistles are all lures when autumn comes, and if you can strike a balance between your love of birds and your natural gardener's pride, a smattering of weeds will encourage smaller, shyer birds and those that feed on the insects which, in turn, favour the weeds. Cooked, fatty scraps and crumbs encourage many birds, as do nuts.

Large birds such as the green woodpecker (*Picus viridis*) (Plate 16) may choose to make a particular garden their territory for a number of reasons, often to the benefit of the gardener, as they rid the lawn of grubs, ants and other insects. The flash of a bright yellow rump and sudden cackling laugh – the 'yaffle' of its country name – as a woodpecker flits from lawn to perch can become a familiar and well-loved feature of an open, airy garden. Though shy of too close a human contact, woodpeckers are often static long enough to be well observed from a window – and large enough to allow quick and easy sketching.

◀ *PLATE 16*

The green woodpecker is a bird of many names: yaffle, rain-bird (in some areas its call is believed to herald the coming of a downpour) and most delightfully, popinjay – in medieval and later times the name given to a conceited young dandy. Certainly the bird's bright plumage gives him that jaunty, devil-may-care aspect, especially during courtship when the male pursues his mate with an elaborate ritual dance, spiralling around tree trunks, raising his crest and flipping his wing tips.

When colours blend together softly, such as on the breast where green gives way to cream, try using the appropriate shades together in the needle in the 'transition' strata between one and the next.

Embroidery shown actual size
21.5 x 21.5cm (8½ x 8½in)

PLATE 17 ▶
Part of a larger study, this middle distance 'sketch' of a heron captures all the essentials of the bird in fine, impressionistic stitching. As the bird rises from the water it has not yet assumed its usual leisurely flight, legs stretched elegantly behind it – the undercarriage is still down! It can be a useful trick to work a small area of blue sky or cloud just behind the moving object to suggest a distant perspective and give the subject a 'location' in even the most open setting. Use very fine horizontal stitching and don't be tempted to over-do it.
Dimensions of bird and cloud
10.25 x 6.5cm (4 x 2½in)

The broad expanse of uninterrupted colour on a woodpecker's upper body, flecked only by spotting lower down, provides a perfect example of the fluidity of radial *opus plumarium* as a medium in which to capture this spectacular bird. As greens, greys and whites give way to the red and black moustache and other head markings, the overall flow of the stitches is unbroken – the sweep of the feathers complete. If you are lucky enough to find a discarded tail feather examine it closely; it is, in turn, a perfect example of the principles of directional *opus plumarium*. Art must imitate nature!

A less welcome, though equally impressive, visitor to any garden that boasts a fish pond is the grey heron (*Ardea cinerea*), shown in Plate 17. Like the magpie (*Pica pica*) (Fig 11), the heron is an opportunist predator and once a likely source of food has been established it will return again and again until the unfortunate victims, whether fish or young birds, are decimated. Its lugubrious, heavy-flapping flight makes it a good subject for a distant sketch that can be included in the middle background of a larger study using the principles of miniaturisation (see Chapter Two).

Less destructive and easier to attract to the garden are the smaller birds – thrushes, tits, and other 'bird-table' visitors. In spring there is nothing more glorious than to enjoy the dawn chorus in the knowledge that the cast will be attending the post-performance breakfast in full view of a still-appreciative audience. The song thrush (*Turdus philomelos*) (Fig 12) lives up to its name superbly, and as well as quietly enjoying the usual bird-table treats, often provides a splendid secondary entertainment in the percussion section as it smashes snails on a favourite stone – its own anvil chorus.

◀ *FIG 11*

A single magpie is considered to bring ill luck but any magpie is bad news for eggs and fledglings of smaller birds. Try sketching in pastels: they have an affinity with embroidery in that colours can be easily mixed. Here, the pure black plumage of the magpie's upper body merges into the blue and green-black of its wings and tail. Sketch initially in black, overlay a colour and blend together with a finger – it's rather like mixing colours in your needle.

Blue tits (*Parus caeruleus*) (Plate 18) are even easier to observe. In an urban courtyard or cottage garden, whether in winter or summer, the blue tit's antics are always a source of delight. Milk bottle tops present it with little challenge in the quest for cream, nuts hung at any angle are an invitation to dine, and in spring adults make short work of any number of less-than-garden-friendly grubs and caterpillars as they feed a voracious brood of up to fourteen chicks. When the chicks fledge the entertainment continues; for several weeks the family stays together and sometimes joins with other groups to form a gregarious, noisy band of youngsters, in turns garrulous and sleepy.

Plate 18 is inspired by the charming little family that emerged from my own bird box one spring. The siblings would separate into intimate

◀ *FIG 12*

Thrushes, like blackbirds, listen for worms and other prey moving beneath the grass, then a tug-of-war may begin between bird and hapless victim. Here, again, pastels make for easy sketching of a design that can be brought back to the drawing board for transfer. Colour in the breast and belly in a pale shade and smudge darker brown spots over the top – these will translate into Dalmatian dog spots during embroidery.

▶ *PLATE 18*

'Two little Dickie birds . . .' It is tempting, at first glance, to look at these two blue tit babies as mirror images, but in fact there are a number of differences, apart from the obvious sleepiness of the right-hand chick. As well as the inescapable variance that comes with freehand sketching at design stage, an awareness of the 'imagined light source' means that the highlighting of the breast feathers must be carefully worked when the embroidery is completed. This, of course, is echoed in the light/dark sides of the directional opus plumarium *on the leaves. A study such as this should be framed simply, to concentrate the eye on the image itself.*

10.25 x 6.5cm (4 x 2½in)

groups of two or three to chatter or snooze between feeds, for all the world like little old men on a park bench. To capture the charm of young birds be particularly careful in your choice of colours. Fledglings tend toward more pastel shades (even browns are often paler and more mottled) and feather out the edges of each contour to suggest the downy, immature nature of the plumage. The closed eye of the chick to the right is suggested by two tiny arcs of directional stitching separated by a line of black (no highlight of course) in contrast to the beady, wide-awake eye of the left-hand bird. Here the eye ring is picked out carefully in a fine stem stitch to separate the eye itself from the supercilium. A simple twig and a few bright green spring leaves are all that is needed to complete the study.

In general, the smaller the bird, and the more close-up our study, the more detailed our interpretation of the various features needs to be. In Plate 18 great attention has been paid to the subtle shading of the breasts – from creamy yellow to near white and back to yellow. In Plate 19, a little Jenny Wren (*Troglodytes troglodytes*) sports much more intricate markings, although on a body little bigger than the young tits. Here we must begin to apply the principles of Dalmatian dog spotting, shooting stitches and ticking on a smaller scale than we have so far explored.

Whether on a large or small subject the principles of all our basic techniques remain the same (as we have discussed with regard to miniaturisation), their application, however, must vary to suit the needs of the individual project. Sweeping radial *opus plumarium* over the neck and down the head of the mallard (Plate 10) or directional *opus plumarium* along the shafts of the magnificent flight feathers of the barn owl (Plate 15), we have been able to use relatively long stitches. These are regulated only by the need to change colour or by the degree of the curve being described. On a small subject, the length of the stitches must be determined by the same criteria but, naturally, will be reduced by the ratio of the size differential. We will be practising these skills in Masterclass Three.

The wren is a pert little bird, all jaunty angles and precise, crisp brown markings. As with larger subjects, the core of the stitching is at the tip of the beak, and the directional flow must be aligned accordingly. The size of the stitches, however, should be appropriately delicate – the approximate length of the strata needed to describe the curve of the forehead, crown and nape can be identified easily by the length of the stitches creating the supercilium – a paler flash through the surrounding brown.

▲ *PLATE 19*

Forsythia is one of the first brightly flowering shrubs of the spring and a welcome perch during the wren's early courtship. Small insects, gnats and spiders are favourite foods, though seeds may augment the diet. A fresh dimension is given to this study with the addition of a few tiny, roughly cut semiprecious stones at the base of the forsythia branch. Peridot and citrine, these stones echo the colours of the embroidery and provide a small but definite suggestion of the inner dimensions of the study – they form the angle of a corner.

11.5 x 10.25cm (4½ x 4in)

▶ *FIG 13*

The robin redbreast is Christmas personified. At drawing board stage a simple sketch can be given your own 'shorthand' treatment by suggesting the length of the various strata needed to complete the radial opus plumarium. *If you wish, you can transfer these on to your fabric – they will ultimately be covered by embroidery. Create your template in a manner that suits your own work style.*

Using the same principle, all the other techniques should be similarly minimised: the length of the central shafts on the flight feathers, the size of shooting and ticking stitches, even the seed stitch that forms the highlight of the eye. Fine work can be made easier by making sure that you are working in a good light and it is essential that you choose needles that are fine enough to allow accurate positioning (see notes on tools in Materials, page 89.)

Like the robin (*Erithacus rubecula*) (Fig 13), and the house sparrow (*Passer domesticus*) (Plate 20), the wren is one of Britain's most familiar garden birds. It is resident in the cooler and more temperate regions of North America, where it is also a welcome visitor to the bird-table. It is almost as prolific at the blue tit – though with a different and highly original life style. The male builds several nests, only one of which is chosen by the female, into which she lays and incubates up to eight eggs. When the chicks fledge, the father may take them to one of the 'alternative' nests to be nurtured by him for a little longer while the female lays another clutch of eggs and begins the rearing process again.

Although often tempted to the bird-table, the wren is basically a shy bird – its plumage is a masterpiece of camouflage, all mottled browns, greys and buffs, perfectly suited to its chosen habitat in dense hedgerows and scrubby undergrowth. The house sparrow – though certainly not shy to the same extent – sports a similar livery, though unlike the wren the sexes are quite different.

There were probably no house sparrows in the British Isles before man: they are thought to have arrived when our Neolithic ancestors arrived from continental Europe. Certainly there were originally none in North America where they were introduced by European settlers but have now spread widely. A true opportunist, the sparrow has made the most of its relationship with man – feeding off his grain fields and nesting in the warmth of his buildings. The cheeky 'Cockney Sparrer' was considered in 1961 when the International Council for Bird Preservation was set the task of choosing Britain's national bird. Only after long consideration was the accolade given to the robin. Perhaps the latter's more colourful markings won the day, for the sparrow is often considered to be a dull-looking bird, though when examined closely the subtleties and intricacies of its plumage are delightful. The gaudy head-dress and flashy body plumage of occasional visitors such as the hoopoe (*Upupa epops*) (Fig 14) seem brash by comparison.

In Masterclass Three, the various markings of the male and female house sparrow provide us with all the practise we need to become confident in the description of small birds, from scaled-down Dalmatian dog spotting to the closely abutted stem stitch needed to reflect the wing markings. The stance of small birds is often the main element of their jizz – delicate toes and claws can cling on to lightweight supports that allow full view of the bird. Working the legs will be explored fully at details 3 and 4. Finally, a colourful setting is an advantage – the pelargoniums of many a cottage window-sill or courtyard flower-pot are a perfect foil. The bright, broad swathes of colour on both flowers and leaves present a counterpoint to the fine, detailed marking of the birds. Add the flight of a holly blue butterfly and the summer-time comes flooding into the dullest winter day.

▲ *FIG 14*

The extraordinary crest of the hoopoe gives him the appearance of a Red Indian chief! As a rare visitor to Britain he is something of a star, drawing 'twitchers' from all over the country. Even in a rough sketch, a suggestion of blue sky gives a distant perspective to a study, while dancing gnats in the foreground bring the main subject closer to the viewer.

House Sparrows

Chestnut brown and pure white, with a smart little black bib, the male house sparrow is quite a contrast to his rather more dappled and muted mate. The female's light brown upper body and beige grey underparts provide her with supreme camouflage, but are a pretty study in themselves. Pelagonium 'Wembley Gem' provides a colourful counterbalance.

This study could be striking if worked on a black background. The black 'bib' would need to be highlighted (see step 3, Masterclass Four) and touches of gold metallic thread could be included – for example on the 'whiskers' of the grasses. On a pale background, as illustrated here, the design is light and airy.

Dalmatian dog spotting is an important feature of these house sparrows and true radial *opus plumarium* (falling back to a central rather than a displaced core) forms the primary technique for both the flowers and zonal leaves of the pelargoniums. A quick re-cap of these skills in the Stitch Variations section might be useful. If you wish to replace the butterfly with an alternative motif, remember to include the changes at template stage.

TECHNIQUES

Filling and linear techniques form the basis of this study:

Stem stitch • Radial *opus plumarium*

Dalmatian dog technique • Snake stitch

Straight stitch • Seed stitch

PLATE 20 ▶

Masterclass Three: Embroidery shown actual size 23 x 21.5cm (9 x 8½in)

HELEN M.
STEVENS

Fine details, such as the grass's whiskers and the legs of the greenfly are added freehand later – they do not appear on the template. Features within a field of stitching, such as the zonal demarcations on the foliage and the Dalmatian spots on the birds' plumage are hidden by the embroidery so they can be traced and transferred.

Remember that the annotated colours on the chart are for reference only – refer to Plate 20 when choosing your shades. In places, for example on the female's head, the specified colour has actually been achieved by mixing two shades in the needle. If your thread is fine enough why not try creating the same effect? If you are using a broader gauge, simply choose a shade that captures the overall colour scheme. If you decide to replace the butterfly with another motif, use colours that do not clash with the rest of the study.

Suggested Colours

1 Black
2 Grey
3 Beige grey
4 White
5 Light brown
6 Chestnut brown
7 Light green
8 Salmon pink
9 Dark green
10 Yellow-green
11 Gold
12 Blue

DESIGN NOTES

The imagined light source in this study is from the top right-hand quarter. To simplify the sequential instructions it is assumed that the order of working each bird is roughly similar: e.g., step 1, as it is applied to the female is repeated on the male – with the appropriate substitution of colours and so on. The later techniques as they are applied to the male are also relevant to the female.

BEGIN WITH SHADOW LINING . . .

Work smooth or fragmented shadow lining throughout in black (1).

1 Generally applicable to both birds: infill the eye with black straight stitching and work the beak in grey (2) radial stitching converging upon its tip. Work short strata of radial *opus plumarium* in the appropriate shades of brown – light brown (5) or chestnut (6) – over the head, the smaller markings in black and the cheeks and ear coverts in white (4).

Begin to work down the breast in beige grey (3) or black. Work Dalmatian dog spots on the upper backs and flood light or chestnut brown around them. On the female work the two upper wing bars in black and white respectively. Use straight stitches in beige grey to describe the central shafts of the wing feathers.

2 Both birds: complete the fine details of the face – the eye ring and highlight in white. Continue working down the back and rump, flooding around Dalmatian dog spots and changing shade where appropriate. Similarly work down the breast, belly and undertail coverts, maintaining the flow of the *opus plumarium* through the various changes of shade. Merge the leg feathers into the belly plumage.

Male wings: work the primary coverts in snake stitch in chestnut brown, voiding slightly between each feather. On the upper three flight feathers work a fine inner line of fairly broad stem stitch in black. Infill with directional *opus plumarium* in chestnut brown.

Female wings: work the primary coverts similarly in light brown and the flight feathers with an inner line of black stem stitch, infilled with light brown directional work. Repeat these techniques for the long tail feathers.

3 Pay particular attention to the shadow line on the legs, then in beige grey work the legs in carefully angled snake stitch. Try to follow the contour of the anatomy – where the toes separate, sweep the stitches around smoothly without breaking the directional flow.

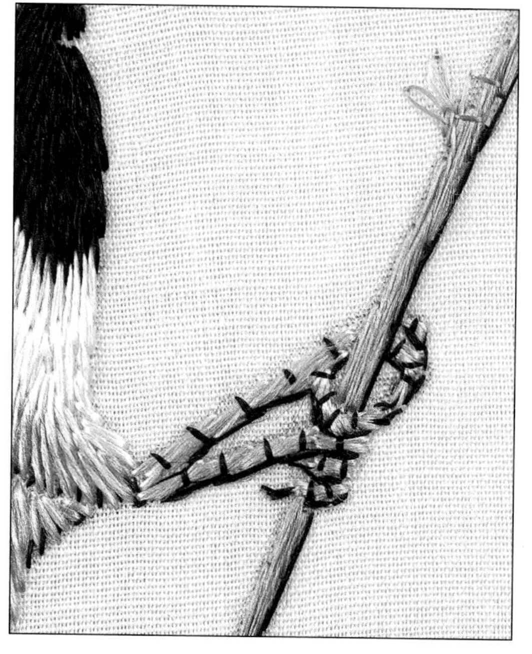

4 To create the 'wrinkled stockings' effect, use a fine black thread to work short straight stitches across the snake stitch, at right angles to the parallel outlines of the legs and toes. Work the claws in two or three graduating stem stitches in fine black.

Using any very fine yellow-green (10) thread, create the greenfly with a few straight stitches to form a round body, two lazy-daisy stitches for wings and a few random straight stitches to suggest legs.

Moving On To The Pelargoniums . . .

5 In light green (7) snake stitch work the main stems of the flower heads and the stalks of the buds in stem stitch. In the same shade create the sepals of the opening buds and the entire closed buds in lozenges of radial *opus plumarium*.

Work each petal in a single stratum of radial *opus plumarium* in salmon pink (8) falling back to a central core. Where the petals of each floret converge, work seed stitches in light green.

Complete each multiple flower head by adding the emerging petals of the buds in part lozenges of radial work in salmon pink.

6 Work the leaf stalks in snake stitch and the converging veins of each leaf in stem stitch in light green (top right). Then (anticlockwise) in radial *opus plumarium*, work an inner stratum in light green, a middle stratum in dark green (9) and an outer stratum in light green. Referring to Plate 20, complete the long blades of grass in snake stitched yellow-green and the stalks of the grass heads in the same shade in stem stitch. Following the colour chart, work the grains in lozenges of radial *opus plumarium* in gold (11) and light brown respectively. Tip each grain with a long, straight stitched whisker in gold.

Moving On To The Butterfly . . .

7 Work the straight stitched body and the broad inner strata of the wings in blue (12).

Blend the narrow outer strata of black and white respectively and add the antennae in long straight stitches tipped with clubs of short straight stitches in fine black.

Add your own touches at the foot of the composition – long, straight stitched grasses and horizontal stitching to suggest a base element.

HELEN M.
STEVENS

CHAPTER FOUR

WATER BIRDS

The quicksilver flash of a fish, the even faster dash and splash of turquoise lightning as a kingfisher dives into the shot-silk blue and white of a rippling stream, and there is food again for a hungry brood.

With up to seven youngsters per clutch to feed, kingfishers have a busy season throughout the summer. Two broods are the norm and in Britain from April to August, incubating eggs, nurturing young nestlings or feeding the still-needy fledglings takes up all the adults' time. Autumn is perhaps a time for some leisure, but in a hard winter the kingfisher is again far from easy street – frozen water means a freeze on foodstuff as the small fish that are the bird's staple diet are inaccessible. Many kingfishers retreat to coastal creeks and rock pools where they have a better chance of survival.

On a personal level, the kingfisher has a very special place in my heart – it was the bird featured on the cover of my first book and has become almost synonymous with the use of *opus plumarium*. Its shape, colouring and jaunty, confident jizz make it a gift to embroiderers: front or rear aspect, in flight or perching, the kingfisher is the perfect subject. Tastes do not seem to have changed over the generations. At the turn of the twelfth and thirteenth centuries the monk Giraldus described the 'Halcyon' birds that appeared in illuminated manuscripts as being, 'strikingly beautiful . . . red breast and reddish beak and feet, back and wings gleaming bright green like a parrot or peacock'. Embroideries of the same era must have reflected similar effects (see Introduction, page 5). Not all birds though were so easily identified (see Fig 15 overleaf).

Plate 21 captures not just the adult but also the young birds: plumage slightly

◄ *PLATE 21*

The kingfisher held a fascination for the ancients that far pre-dates the Anglo-Saxons. According to Greek mythology the halcyon bird could control the winds and the water and was much respected by sailors as a bird of the goddess Athene. It was said to build a floating nest of fish bones and nurture its young at sea, keeping the waters calm by magic. Its spectacular colouring was also a gift of the gods. After the biblical Flood, the kingfisher was sent to fetch fire from heaven. Lightning struck its back – hence the blue flash – and the fire burnt its breast red! Happily it suffers less vicissitudes in real life: its flesh tastes unpleasantly bitter and it is rarely sought as prey.

Embroidery shown actual size

21 x 23cm (8¼ x 9in)

▲ *FIG 15*
The moorhen (Gallinula chloropus) *(left) takes its name from the Anglo-Saxon word* 'mor' *meaning mere or bog and can be confused with the coot* (Fulica atra) *but for the birds' respective red and white foreheads. The expression 'bald as a coot' has entered the language (see also Plate 13), though of course the bird is not really tonsorially challenged!*

rougher, beaks and feet slightly more mottled, they will be fed by their parents until they are able to fish for themselves. Like many water birds, the kingfisher's shape and its overall plumage is streamlined, but its feathers have no special waterproofing. Their plunge underwater normally lasts less than a second, so a quick shake of the feathers and all is back to normal. Apart, therefore, for a demarcation of the primary flight feathers and a suggestion of the coverts, the main body of the bird is described by smooth radial *opus plumarium* – converging upon the long, spear-like beak. The adult and left-hand chick have beaks slightly open, the former holding food, the latter ready to receive it. Remember, though, these are not secondary cores but rather a single, primary core of the stitching, split to allow reality into a study. Your stitches should still flow smoothly.

Ticking is the principle decorative technique used in Plate 21. On the forehead, crown and nape, lower moustache, shoulder and upper wing, the underlying *opus plumarium* is highlighted by ticking stitches in ice blue. In the middle and background of the study, horizontal, angled and perpendicular straight stitching suggest the river and banks, whilst the pollarded willow is capped with seed stitched foliage. Seed stitches are also used to describe the distant irises.

Deciding what 'incidental' motifs should be included in a large study is an art in itself. To the right of the action in Plate 21, two long, linear leaves frame the overall roundel of the main design. Similarly in Plate 22 the young avocets are balanced by two fronds of snake stitching creating a designated border. Features such as these, whether on a pale or dark background, help to 'finish' a design and direct the eye back to the main subject.

The avocet (*Recurvirostra avosetta*) is an amazing story of bird preservation. By 1825 it was declared extinct in Britain after the last pairs were wiped out – their feathers were sought for fishing flies, their eggs for a special pudding. After the Second World War a few birds, dislodged from their habitual nest sites in the Netherlands by the hostilities, began to nest again on the east coast of England. The Royal Society for the Protection of Birds secured and protected the breeding sites, adopted the bird as its logo, breeding pairs

◀ *PLATE 22*

The old country name of the avocet is 'yelper' – rather undignified for such an attractive bird but evidence of the loud yelp emitted when it is disturbed. In calmer moments it expresses a more modern outlook and coos 'cool-it'! In the young birds, the adult avocet's upturned bill is less apparent – food is sought by sweeping the bill back and forth through the shallows to catch small water creatures.

Horizontal straight stitching is worked either with or without voiding, respectively, to create the impression of water seeping into the sand, or small stones rising above the flats.

10.25 x 10.75cm (4 x 4¼in)

increased rapidly and ever since the avocet has been a symbol of the tenacity – given the chance – of even the shyest bird.

The chicks in Plate 22 are typical of all young birds in that their plumage is downier, their stance gawkier and their charm, if anything, even greater than that of their parents. The former as been achieved by simply feathering out fine straight stitches on the belly and undertail coverts, the next by design and the last by relying upon the innate appeal of the subject itself! The long, sharply angled beak of many water birds makes the flow of the radial work easy to follow, as here. Occasionally, though, the pattern is less easy to follow.

In Fig 16 three water birds demonstrate the sweep of the stitching. The yellow wagtail

▲ *FIG 16*

*In each of these birds 'x' marks the core or growing point. On the upper two birds, yellow wagtail (*Motacilla flava*) and dipper (*Cinclus cinclus*), the simple flow of the stitches is shown by the white-headed arrows. Black-headed arrows on the ruddy duck (*Oxyura jamaicensis*) chart the more complicated flow of the contours and hence, of course, the stitches.*

and the dipper (top and middle) have beaks tapering to a fine, straight tip. However, the ruddy duck (below) has a puffed-up breast, a rounded, sloping forehead and a concave curve to the top of its bill. Before taking your first stitch STOP, THINK and ANALYZE your design (STAy). Only when you are sure of the flow of the stitches, certain of the way each plane blends into the next should you begin to embroider. 'STAy' is a good acronym to use before you begin any complicated project. More stitches are unpicked, more projects left unfinished and more embroiderers frustrated by rushing in without 'staying' a moment to examine the exercise, than ever were by hesitation. Plate 23 is a case in point.

The exquisite little egret (*Egretta garzetta*) of southern Europe and north Africa (also parts of Australia) is closely related to the North American snowy egret. All egrets grow glorious, feathery plumes or *aigrettes* during the mating season. This finery was very nearly their nemesis at the turn of the last century as thousands of birds were slaughtered to satisfy the demands of the fashion trade: hats and capes, bags and coats were all likely to be adorned to the detriment of these unfortunate birds. At first glance the long whip-like feathering of the back and coverts seems an inextricable mass of spaghetti, but if we 'STAy' for a moment we can begin to unravel the picture.

Beak, head, neck and back are worked to the usual principles of radial *opus plumarium*, even the crest plumes seem to sweep easily toward the overall flow. Where the long, plumed feathers begin to overlay the rest of the body (like a flapper's fringed dress) we must begin to pay particular attention. First (if working on a pale background), shadow line each plume. Then work each plume, in either stem or snake stitch, depending upon the width of the field – reflexing or simple as appropriate (see Stitch Variations, page 93). When these main arcs have been worked, fill in the plumage of the body, working around and voiding between each previously worked feature. Finally, feather out the plumes by overlaying fine straight stitches at angles that correspond to the various arcs already worked. Where lower body and legs become an integral part of the foreground features of flowers and foliage, gradually allow the two to become merged (see Masterclass Four).

◀ *PLATE 23*

Part of a larger study, this egret stands sentinel over the rice plains of Italy. Yellow flag irises mass around the base of the design and hide much of the bird's legs. A subliminal suggestion of the colour of the legs, however, is given by working a few straight stitches in the appropriate shade and direction amongst the foliage and flowers. This is just enough to create the impression of the feature without 'confusing' the foreground elements. This device is used again in Plate 25 (Masterclass Four).
14 x 25.5cm (5½ x 10in)

▲ *FIG 17*

A typical jizz of the pretty roseate tern shows the bird snuggled down into her scrape (nest) of pebbles. Suggest all 'ground' features with horizontal stitching and all 'growing' features with roughly perpendicular work. A quick couple of arrows at the sketching stage can be a useful reminder later.

Water birds seem to be particularly prone to ill-use by man – whether through war, peacetime fashion-victim, prosperity or holiday exuberance. The roseate tern (*Sterna dougallii*) (Fig 17), along with others in the tern family, have found breeding sites disturbed since annual seaside holidays became the norm. One group of birds, though – the gull family – has played man at his own game, and won. Whether at sea or on land, gulls use man's ingenuity to their own ends, scavenging after the fishing fleet and the farmer's plough, equally at ease with a diet of fish or worms and insects. In Plate 24 they form a counterpoint of action against the eerie stillness of a solar eclipse. This picture was commissioned after a client had witnessed the last total eclipse of the twentieth century. It is a sombre, inspiring and almost frightening moment. Suddenly the mood lifts as, bemused by the thought that night has fallen so quickly, a slightly comical formation of gulls sweeps across the bay – somehow normality is restored.

Miniaturisation is again brought into play here. The gulls are pared down to their base essentials – working on a black background, even the shadow line is omitted, but the vigour, movement and characteristic jizz in flight is retained. In what medium other than embroidery could a few stitches convey a questing beak and heavy, pendant feet as on the bird to the far right? Cellophane thread creates the beams of fragmented light and loose, unspun silk suggests the fine high clouds (see *The Myth and Magic of Embroidery* and *Helen M. Stevens' World of Embroidery* for a full explanation of these techniques).

Working a landscape on a black ground fabric produces a striking, atmospheric effect – more often landscapes are better suited to a pale backdrop. Close-up studies, however, particularly featuring brightly coloured subjects, are frequently seen to their best advantage against black. Often though, especially in the case of natural history studies, certain features are themselves black. This creates a dilemma – how are we to emphasise black embroidery against a self-coloured background? Working floss silk on a basically mat fabric (such as polycotton) the difference in texture is evident, but this is not always enough to delineate a feature. Highlighting, then, is the answer.

◀ *PLATE 24*

In the subdued lighting of the solar eclipse, the seagulls are worked in an eye-catching white and blue-grey floss silk. They appear to catch and refract the light 'within' the study, just as they do the 'real' light. Take a little time when deciding where to hang your finished work: if the primary daytime light source comes from a window, you may wish to position your work so that it catches light at an angle rather than from directly opposite. This will enhance the effect of the directional stitching. Make sure though that the embroidery is never in full sunlight.

23 x 18cm (9 x 7in)

In Plate 25 a pair of beautiful, great crested grebes (*Podiceps cristatus*) and their young are worked against black. The surrounding features are kept simple, the attention focused on the finery of the birds themselves, including their glossy black crests and ruffs. Working in the finest white thread possible, a suggestion of light catching the outermost tips of the black feathers is created. Straight stitches are taken at exactly the same angle as the main strata of the stitching, the line of the highlight 'fragmented' to allow the effect of the feathery outline to be maintained. Unlike shadow lining (which should always be completed *before* the main body of the embroidery) highlighting should be added *after* the completion of the last strata. As with any 'finishing touches' the decision of how much or how little of any feature is needed can only be taken when the main body of the work is *in situ*.

Masterclass Four allows you to choose the extent of the surrounding grasses. The legs of the left-hand grebe will be hidden by them: they will 'frame' the action at the bottom of the study. Similarly the dancing gnats at the top of the study could be placed anywhere, omitted entirely or replaced with another fine detail. Don't be afraid to experiment.

▲ *FIG 18*

Less spectacular than its cousin the great crested grebe (Plate 25), the little grebe (Tachybaptus ruficollis) *still makes a pretty subject. Most grebes carry their young on their backs: larger chicks stay close to their parents until fledged. The rougher outline of the sketched baby will translate into equally irregular outer strata of stitching.*

Masterclass Four

GREAT CRESTED GREBES WITH YOUNG

These elegant birds, together with a slightly minimalist setting, create a rather oriental impression. Balanced, and yet asymmetrical, the attitude of the two adult birds is echoed in the chicks at the base of the design – a third takes a ride on its parent's back. Centring its attention on something 'outside' the immediate circle of the family, this chick is an important element in the composition of the piece.

The embroidery is designed to be worked on a dark background. A deep green could be substituted for the black, but shadow lines would confuse the simplicity of the piece, so make sure that your chosen shade is dark enough not to require them. An element of voiding is essential. Work in a good light – this is especially important when working black on black!

Fine details are an integral part of the adult birds' heads – they counterbalance the otherwise simplistic sweep of the plumage. As with the previous Masterclass, work the design sequentially, but bear in mind that instructions relating to one bird are also relevant to the other – they have not necessarily been repeated. Male and female are identical.

TECHNIQUES

This is a return to the use of broad radial stitching – it looks deceptively simple!

Radial *opus plumarium* • Shooting stitch
Straight stitch • Ticking • Studding
Snake stitch • Dalmatian dog technique

PLATE 25 ▶

Masterclass Four: Embroidery shown actual size 22.25 x 20.5cm (8¾ x 8in)

HELEN M.
STEVENS

If you feel it may help with the flow of the radial work, sketch in a few lines to suggest the direction of the stitches. Several of these 'key' lines have been included on the right-hand bird. Refer to Plate 25 to ascertain the correct directional sweep and add the rest yourself – they can be transferred on to your background fabric as they will ultimately be covered by the embroidery.

Suggested Colours

1 Dark grey
2 Black
3 Orange-red
4 White
5 Orange
6 Old gold
7 Pale grey
8 Gold
9 Light brown
10 Dark brown
11 Medium brown
12 Cream
13 Dark blue
14 Light blue
15 Light green
16 Dark green

It is a feature of broad radial opus plumarium *that a simple design may need a considerable number of colours to create effective shading (see Masterclass One). In Plate 25, shade 11 (medium brown) has been achieved by mixing shades 9 and 10 in the needle – as discussed in Masterclass Three. If you have a variety of thread types at your disposal, try using floss for the birds, twisted silk for the water and a mat cotton (stranded is ideal) for the grasses.*

Design Notes

The imagined light source in this study is coming from directly above the subject. Pay particular attention to this when it comes to highlighting 'black against black' features.

Begin With The Adult Grebes . . .

1 Work the beak in radial *opus plumarium*, tapering toward the tip in dark grey (1), the pupil of the eye in a few short straight stitches in black (2) and the iris in a tiny circle of radial *opus plumarium* in orange-red (3).

In graduating strata of radial *opus plumarium* complete the face in pale grey (7), black and white (4), blending the work smoothly into the cheek and ear covert in orange (5).

Sweep the stitches up and out to create the near-side crest in black, and continue down the back of the head. Void between this area and the cheek and ear covert. Work the far crest in the same directional sweep and void appropriately.

2 Continue the radial *opus plumarium* to complete the head. In the same technique work the nape of the neck in old gold (6) and the throat in white. Void between this area and the head, but allow the colours to blend smoothly where neck meets throat.

Begin to work the fine details of the face: a long straight stitch in black through the beak, between upper and lower mandible and a few shooting stitches (also in black) to create a fine eye line below the small pale grey strata.

3 Complete the fine details on the head and highlight the eye with a seed stitch in white. Work fine shooting stitches in orange to subdue the void between the ear covert/cheek area and the black at the back of the head. Extend this to the area between the head and throat. Highlight the 'black against black' outer strata of the work in a very fine white thread. Work short straight stitches at the same angle as the existing strata.

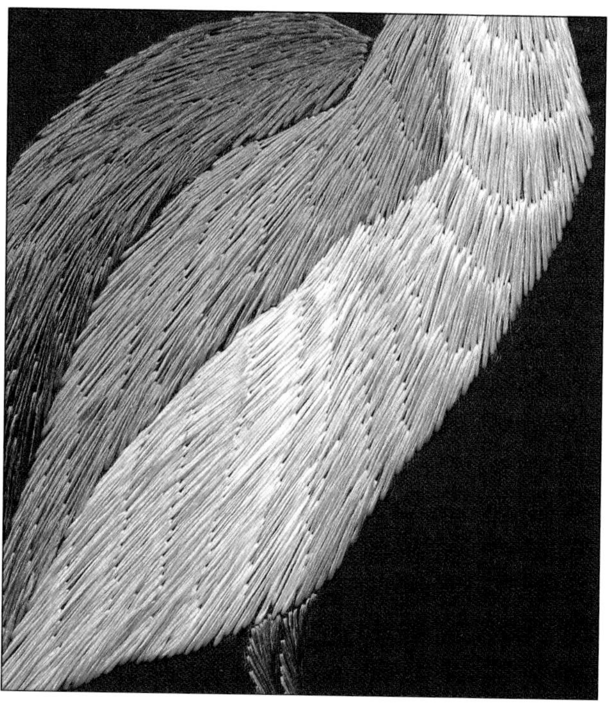

4 Extend the radial *opus plumarium* down the body of the bird in the appropriate shades, blending or abutting the strata as applicable.

Upper body: light brown (9), dark brown (10).

Middle body: old gold, gold (8), old gold.

Lower body: white, pale grey, white, cream (12).

Soften the areas where strata abut with fine shooting stitches (refer to Plate 25). Work a suggestion of the legs in pale brown snake stitch.

5 Returning to the first bird, work the back in smooth strata of radial *opus plumarium*, using light brown, medium brown (11) and dark brown. Work the lower body in cream, sweeping the stitches around to converge upon the rump. Soften the abutting, differently aligned strata with fine shooting stitches in dark brown, and similarly subdue the void up the middle of the back. Work the water in straight horizontal stitching in dark blue (13) and light blue (14) as appropriate.

Moving On To The Chicks . . .

6 Right-hand chick: work the beak in a small wedge of radial *opus plumarium*, the legs in fine snake stitch in dark grey and the eye in a few straight stitches in black. Work two Dalmatian dog spots in orange-red on the forehead and inner cheek. Flood radial work in pale grey around all the features, voiding between the wing and the body and so on. Begin the feather markings by working studding on the head in black. Left-hand chick: continue the markings down the neck and back, gradually changing from studding to ticking. Refer to the illustration for correct positioning of the stitches. Work the chick on its parent's back in the same way.

7 Suggest long grasses and so on, at the base of the design by working perpendicular straight stitching, angled toward its base, using light green (15) and dark green (16) as you choose. Allow these stitches to mass around the legs of the standing bird to soften their outline.

Finally, work a few dancing gnats, a butterfly, more grasses to the right of the design – make the picture your own.

HELEN M
STEVENS

CHAPTER FIVE

FLIGHTS OF FANCY

The Phoenix, its egg hatching from the embers of its own pyre; the Roc, in Arab folklore so large that it could carry an elephant in its talons; the Garuda, the Indian 'bird of life' blotting out the sun with its scarlet, gold and white plumage – the fabulous tapestry of mythology is shot through with mystical birds . . .

And yet there is nothing more wonderful in fiction than the reality of the peacock (*Pavo cristatus*) (Plate 26), related though it is to the humble farmyard chicken and common pheasant (see Chapter One). The peafowl has been domesticated for millennia: originally a native of the Indian sub-continent it was well known by the Greeks and Romans for whom it was attendant upon the goddess Juno or Hera. The Bible tells us that when King Solomon built his temple in 1000BC he imported the peacock into the Holy Land, and ever since it has been the favoured ornamental bird for palaces, shrines and pleasure gardens, and an inspiration to artists in all genre.

Peacocks were appearing in European illuminated manuscripts as early as the late seventh century, a hint perhaps as to their use in fine embroidery. Certainly the iridescent properties of their feathers, the texture of their magnificent display plumage and the stylistic potential of their extraordinary overall outline have always made them the perfect subject for interpretation in silk – and today in other specialist fibres. In Plate 26 I have made a study of their most spectacular features.

The peahen, in comparison to her showy mate, is a drab little bird. (This seems to be of little consequence to her sire: I once witnessed a handsome peacock vying with a farmyard cockerel for a plain little hen – clearly he had no appreciation of female beauty!)

◀ *PLATE 26*

Like the other chapter openers throughout this book, this study is composed to the theme of a roundel and the work could be framed with a circular window mount. The main elements are carefully balanced – the peacock himself, with his broad sweep of tail, forming a counterpoint to the large, almost life-sized feather.

Working in pure silk the embroidery already enjoys an iridescent quality similar to the feathers themselves: the addition of a fine metallic gold thread in places is all that is needed. The same study worked in a more mat thread, such as stranded cotton, could be lifted by the addition of a blending filament – rainbow, blue or green cellophane fibres would achieve a very pleasing effect.

Embroidery shown actual size
22.25 x 24.25cm (8¾ x 9½in)

What the peahen lacks, however, is more than compensated for by her companion: metallic turquoise neck, shimmering indigo breast feathers and a bridal train of bright bottle green. What at first appear to be tail feathers – the huge fan of peacock-eye spots raised upon display – are actually elongated upper tail coverts. One of these feathers is interpreted at the right of Plate 26: a long stem stitched shaft is surmounted by four strata of directional *opus plumarium* to create the 'eye', the filigree of the main body of the feather created by floating embroidery (see Stitch Variations, page 92). Top left, one of the half-moon feathers at the extremity of the train is shown in detail – again four strata of directional work cap the plume, with floating embroidery describing the lower shaft.

We often tend to think that only tropical birds have such 'star quality' (Fig 19), but there are many species closer to home that can compete with their exotic

▲ *FIG 19*

*Birds of Paradise may live up to their names – the 'Magnificent' (*Diphyllodes magnificus*), left, and the 'King of Saxony' (*Pteridophora alberti*) – but in reality they are no more difficult to interpret than any garden bird. Here, the flashy head plumes would simply require a stem stitched shaft supporting a series of small lozenges of radial work and the tail feathers two long arcs of snake stitch.*

◀ *FIG 20*

*The great tit (*Parus major*) is a very common garden visitor, but none the less attractive for that. Although at his brightest during the spring, his plumage is still vivid in autumn – here additional motifs are a dried head of cow parsley and the feathery seed head of the traveller's joy. Work the cow parsley head in straight and stem stitch and the traveller's joy in floating embroidery around a seed-stitched core (see Plate 26 and Stitch Variations page 92).*

◀ PLATE 27

The jaunty little firecrest, like the goldcrest, is less often seen than heard. A piping 'zit-zit' is the usual indication that these tiny birds are on the hunt for insects and spiders. The deep green foliage of the Norway spruce is a dense, safe haven. Here it is worked in chevron stitch (see Stitch Variations) with a lighter upper surface to each needle, lower below and a central spine in a mid shade. The immature cones are worked in massed seed stitch, again shaded lighter above and darker beneath. Compare this study to the similar subject on a black background in Plate 1.

10.25 x 9cm (4 x 3½in)

counterparts. The attributes of more familiar species – markings, profile, colour – can often offer an unexpected and vibrant challenge: in his courting plumage of blue cap, yellow waistcoat and green jerkin, the male great tit is an amazingly flashy suitor (Fig 20). The firecrest (*Regulus ignicapillus*) (Plate 27) is one of Europe's smallest birds but also one of its most sparkling jewels; the other is the goldcrest (*Regulus regulus*) (see Plate 2, page 2). Sporting a fiery orange-red crest, snowy-white and jet-black facial markings, Champagne breast and olive green upper body, the firecrest is a subject equally well suited to working on a pale (as here) or dark background fabric. Plate 1 shows a similar firecrest study on black. Nestled in the foliage and immature pine-cones of the Norway spruce, this little gem would rival the most exotic of the New World's humming-birds.

Amongst the humming-birds is, of course, the tiniest of the world's birds, the Cuban bee hummer – the adult is a miniscule 5.7cm (2¼in) long. The ruby-throated humming-

PLATE 28 ▶
Little if any voiding is allowed between the outstretched flight feathers on this ruby-throated humming-bird to suggest the 'blurring' effect that conveys the idea of extreme speed – the swiftness of the wing deceives the eye! Within the open mouths of the hungry chicks a tiny wedge of red describes the inside of the lower mandibles. These are the smallest of the repetitive triangular motifs – angled open wings, open beaks, chicks' bodies, branch and web – that give this study continuity. The surface couched nest is worked over the top of the underlying stitches forming the branch, adding further depth (see text).
9 x 8.25cm (3½ x 3¼in)

bird (*Archilochus colubris*), a resident of the eastern United States and Canada, is a little longer at 9cm (3½in), its chicks just the size of an average thumb-nail (Plate 28). To create an intimate study of such tiny subjects in embroidery *without* miniaturisation is an interesting project. Without a great many surrounding features, that would act as 'controls' to suggest the scale of the main subject, we must somehow emphasise the delicacy of the birds. Bringing in a textured and therefore slightly three-dimensional element – the nest – has this effect.

Male humming-birds are not model spouses. Many are polygamous, few help with the rearing of the young – mating is consummated in the air, after which he tends to lose interest in the partner. The female builds the nest, a neat affair of plant down cleverly held together with cobwebs. As the brood hatches the nest actually expands, the spiders' web acting as an elastic membrane to accommodate the growing family within. The outside of the nest is expertly camouflaged with mosses and lichens. In Plate 28 this effect is achieved by surface couching a fine bouclé silk thread in a meandering, closely abutting pattern. As it curves around to the back of the nestlings the black 'void' gives a sense of depth, the encircling nest protecting the fragile chicks within.

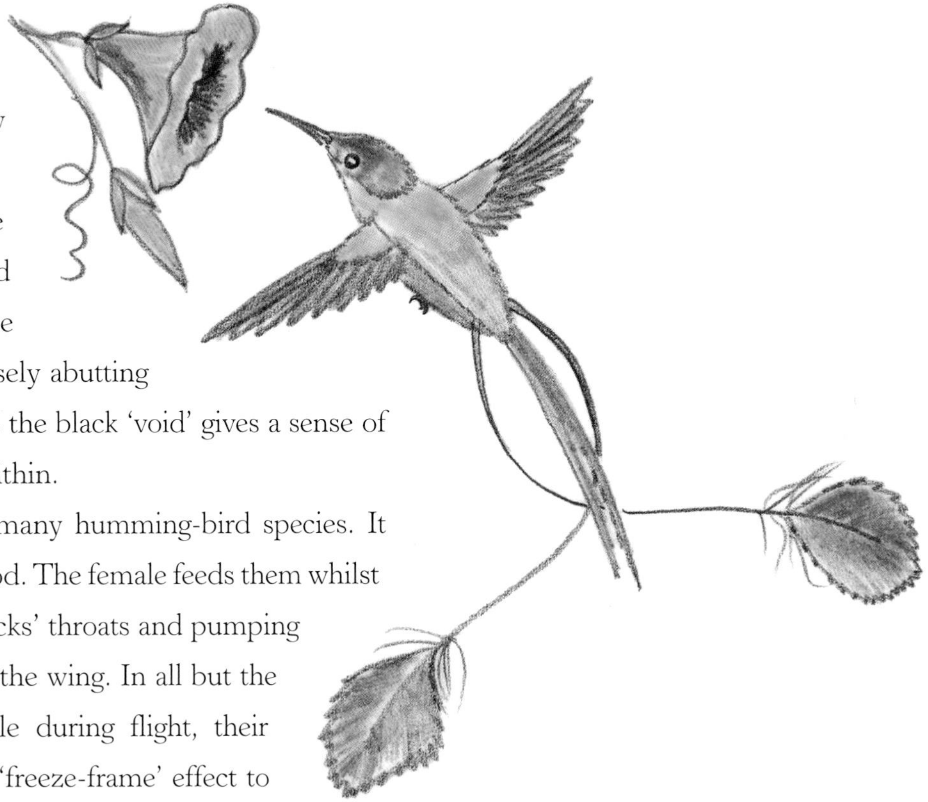

Relatively little is known about the life cycle of many humming-bird species. It seems that there are rarely more than two chicks per brood. The female feeds them whilst hovering, recklessly thrusting her long beak into the chicks' throats and pumping in food. Most of the birds' activities are carried out on the wing. In all but the largest of the species the wings are virtually invisible during flight, their humming beat too fast to be seen. We must achieve a 'freeze-frame' effect to capture the moment. Unlike in the study of a larger bird, however, we can allow the outline of individual feathers to be slightly blurred in recognition of the eye's inability, in reality, to catch such rapid movement.

Fig 21 features Loddiges' racquet-tail (*Loddigesia miralis*), a native of the highlands of northern Peru. The long, racquet-like tail feathers could be approached in the same manner as the large peacock feather in Plate 26: stem stitched shaft, directional *opus plumarium* on the spatula with a fringe of floating embroidery between the two. Fine metallic threads or cellophane-based blending filaments could again be used here to capture the vibrancy of the plumage as discussed at Plate 26.

Just as crests and sparkling highlights are not the prerequisite of tropical species, neither are long tails! The delightful long-tailed tit (*Aegithalos caudatus*) (Plate 29) is, like

▲ *FIG 21*

Humming-birds feed almost exclusively upon the nectar of deep-throated flowers and many species have evolved to be interdependent – the humming-bird pollinates the flower just as bees and other insects do in less exotic circumstances. Humming-birds are featured in depth in Helen M. Stevens' World of Embroidery.

▲ *PLATE 29*

Very careful shadow lining is used in this interpretation of a long-tailed tit (see detail 1, Masterclass Five). Wing markings are delicate and need to be clearly defined before the flight feathers merge into the wing coverts. Here, the tit perches on a broken rose twig. The rosehips are each highlighted by a few strategically placed seed stitches while the thorns are worked in three tiny graduated stem stitches describing a curve, thickening from tip to base – exactly the same technique is used for the bird's claws. In natural history subjects it is not unusual to find very similar motifs used for quite dissimilar purposes. Seed and stem stitches are highly multi-purpose.
10.75 x 10.75cm (4¼ x 4¼in)

the humming-bird, one of the bird world's master builders. Its intricate and unmistakable domed, oval nest boasts a similar outer construction of spiders' web and moss, but inside it is luxury indeed – over 2,000 feathers cushion the young. The fit is so snug that the adults have to fold their tails, which are almost twice the length of their bodies, over their heads when they enter. These pretty little apricot, black and white birds are a joy at any time of the year, either courting, feeding their young or visiting the bird-table on their own account, for they are gregarious and appear to be considerate of each other's space – tails are politely held high so that large numbers of their peers can forage and feed without squabbling.

The little fellow in Plate 29 has focused his attention on the spider's web before him – and its inhabitant. Cobwebs are a useful device in embroidery: they fill a uninteresting corner (as in Plate 28) without making a design too 'busy'; they can be the focal point of a study (as here), or can bring diverse elements together as in Plate 30, Masterclass Five. They can be as large or as small as you choose and the sequence of working is always the same – first the outer framework of the web, then the 'spokes' of the wheel, and finally the web itself, built up concentrically around the middle point. The order of stitching is set out in Fig 22 overleaf.

Tits make excellent models – they are not shy and their acrobatics mean that they are never dull! Even if all you capture in your sketch is a suggestion of bright colour and lively movement, reference to a good field guide will provide you with all the details you need to flesh out your design. The concept will still be yours, so don't be afraid to get out there with your crayons, or to expand your ideas when you get back to the drawing board! You may even find that what begins as a study of birds in your garden turns into something much more unusual.

Plate 30 features birds from both the northern and southern hemispheres (the USA and Australia) and the Orient and yet they are all related to familiar European species.

Clockwise from the top left is the Eastern bluebird (*Sialia sialis*), variegated wren (*Malurus lamberti*), and the varied titmouse (*Parus varius*) – 'bluebirds' all, though technically a thrush, a wren and a tit! In previous Masterclasses we have explored the embroidery of large birds featuring broad swathes of bright colour, and small birds encompassing intricate feather patterns and fine details. Here we put the two concepts together. As in Masterclasses One and Two, smooth radial *opus plumarium* allows colours to blend effectively; the principles of Masterclass Three – the importance of shadow lining (or detailed voiding were the study to be translated on to a black background) – are essential and the freedom of interpretation explored in Masterclass Four allows individuality. Taken step by step these three exotic birds are no more daunting than a common house sparrow.

Throughout this book I have tried to bring to the embroidery of birds a simplicity and spontaneity that is worthy of its subject. Birds far pre-date man in their habitation of our world – they are the natural inheritors of the dinosaurs and masters of air, earth and water. The inspiration that they offered to our ancestors in a multitude of media is still ours for the asking today. Hopefully, we have now come to respect their needs, too. Encouraging birds into our gardens for close-up appreciation is beneficial to both parties, but remember never to venture into breeding sites, interfere with nests or otherwise disturb a bird's natural environment. Lost feathers, hatched eggs and abandoned, fallen nests are all fine source material, but make sure that they can be retrieved without risking their previous owners' well-being. If embroiderers of the future are to have the same wealth of subject matter as we are privileged to enjoy, care must be our watch-word.

In shamanism birds are the vehicles of spiritual flight – guides into the other-world. If this book helps your own embroidery to take wing into flights of both fancy and reality it will have achieved its goal.

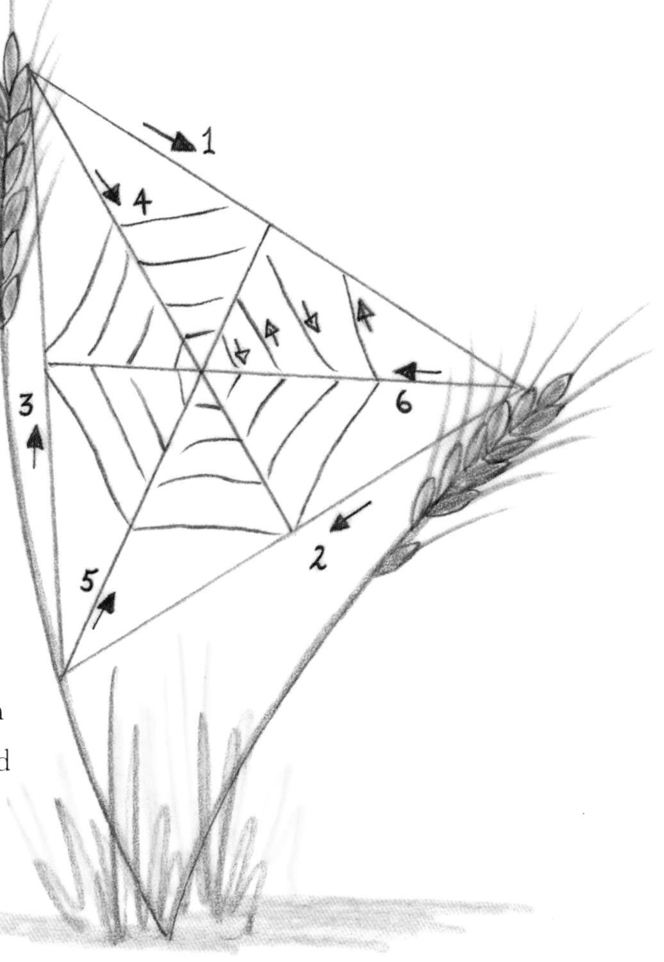

▲ *FIG 22*

Follow the black arrows 1–6 to create the framework and spokes of a spider's web, taking tiny stitches at the back of the fabric, and hiding the thread at the back of the work (behind threads already on the surface) when moving from point to point. Build up the web itself by 'whipping' each spoke (taking the thread through to the back of the fabric) and working around the design in an opposite direction on each circuit (open arrows).

Masterclass Five

'BLUEBIRDS'

With blue as our thematic colour, these birds present three very different challenges – thrush, wren and tit each have their own distinctive jizz and plumage patterns. The four-square stance of the Eastern blue bird, the upturned tail of the variegated wren and the pendant posture of the titmouse are all typical of their respective species. The web and its residents provide a focal point for the subjects and the overall study.

This study could be transposed on to a dark background. If so, the web, should you choose to include it, would be worked in a white or grey thread – as fine as possible – or even a metallic silver thread or blending filament. Grasses and other 'ground-level' features work equally well on a pale or dark background.

Your experience of working previous Masterclasses should now afford you every confidence in completing each of these primary subjects. As before, where one motif has similar attributes to another the design notes apply equally to each – you may need to refer back to a previous motif as you work a later one. Remember to 'STAy' your hand (see page 60) and analyse each subject before you begin.

TECHNIQUES

Many of the most descriptive techniques are reprised in this study:

Stem stitch • Radial *opus plumarium*

Directional *opus plumarium* • Straight stitch

Snake stitch • Ticking

PLATE 30 ▶

Masterclass Five: Embroidery shown actual size 21.5 x 21.5cm (8½ x 8½in)

HELEN M.
STEVENS

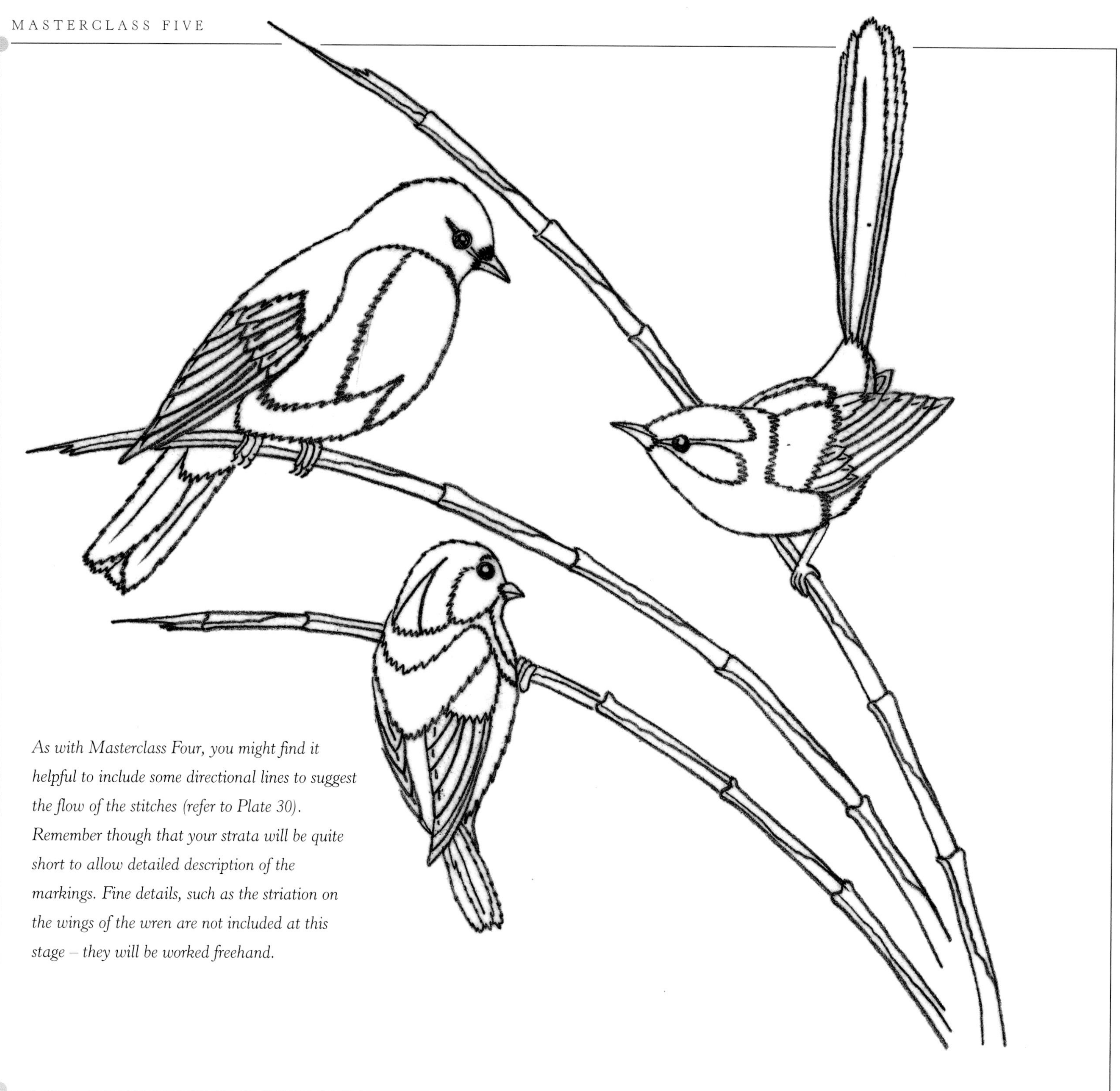

As with Masterclass Four, you might find it helpful to include some directional lines to suggest the flow of the stitches (refer to Plate 30). Remember though that your strata will be quite short to allow detailed description of the markings. Fine details, such as the striation on the wings of the wren are not included at this stage – they will be worked freehand.

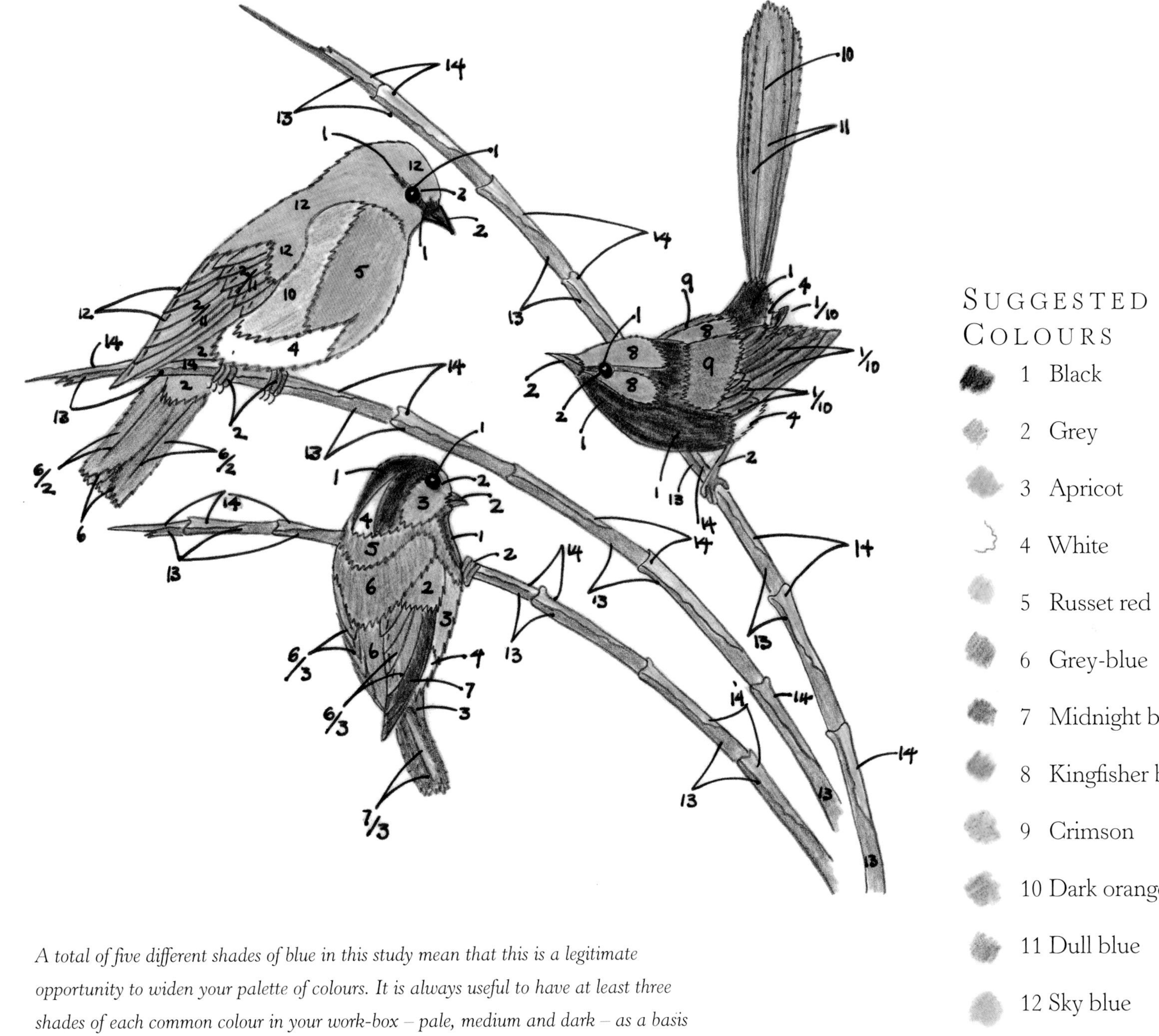

Suggested Colours

1 Black
2 Grey
3 Apricot
4 White
5 Russet red
6 Grey-blue
7 Midnight blue
8 Kingfisher blue
9 Crimson
10 Dark orange
11 Dull blue
12 Sky blue
13 Dark green
14 Light green

A total of five different shades of blue in this study mean that this is a legitimate opportunity to widen your palette of colours. It is always useful to have at least three shades of each common colour in your work-box – pale, medium and dark – as a basis for most designs. When a project appears that needs more unusual tones, acquire specifically what you need. Don't be tempted by too many outlandish shades 'on spec' – they may well lie in your work-box untouched for years!

Design Notes

The imagined light source in this piece originates in the top left-hand quadrant. If you wish to change this alignment – perhaps because you have a definite location in which to display the finished piece – choose it ***now*** *and put a pin in your work pointing in the direction chosen to remind you of the new alignment.*

Begin With The Titmouse . . .

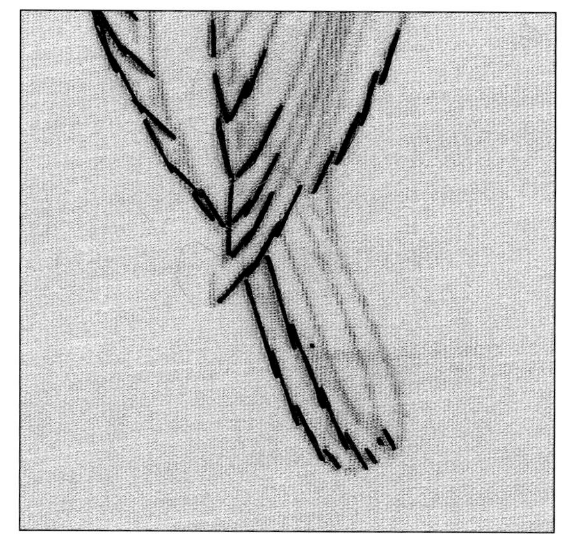

1 Pay particular attention to the shadow lining in black (1) throughout this study. Detailed wing features and separate feathers should all be carefully delineated. If you decide to work the subject on black, remember to void wherever you would have included a shadow line (as well, of course, as on the usual changes of plane).

2 Work delicate wedges of radial *opus plumarium* in grey (2) to create the beak and infill the eye in straight stitched black. Work the forehead and cheek in several strata of radial *opus plumarium* in apricot (3), progressing then to black and white (4) over the head and neck. Highlight the eye with a white seed stitch. Work your way down the breast in strata of black, russet red (5) and apricot and work the back in russet red and grey-blue (6). Complete the wing covert in grey. Three narrow bands of snake stitch in grey are overlaid with black straight stitches for the foot.

Refer to Plate 30 to work the central shafts of flight and tail fathers in straight stitched apricot, surrounding each shaft with strata of directional *opus plumarium* in grey-blue and midnight blue (7) respectively. Work down the breast and undertail covert in apricot, white and apricot strata of radial stitching.

MOVING ON TO THE WREN . . .

3 Complete stages 1 and 2 above in the appropriate shades: the beak in grey; throat, eyeline and so on in black; cheek, ear covert and upper head in kingfisher blue (8); leg in grey and black. Work a fine eye ring in narrow stem stitch in grey (make sure this line is included on each of the birds).

Work the back in strata of kingfisher blue and crimson (9). With a straight stitch in dark orange (10) create the shaft of each primary wing covert feather and work the feathers themselves in black directional *opus plumarium*.

4 Progress down the body of the bird, completing the breast in black, belly in white (refer to Plate 30) and rump in black. Infill the small area of the undertail covert in white. Turning to the wing, work the central shaft of each flight feather in a dark orange straight stitch (upper two feathers), work narrow strata of black directional *opus plumarium* to each side of the shaft (next two feathers) and outer fine strata of directional work in dark orange (bottom three primary feathers). Work obliquely angled strata of directional *opus plumarium* in dull blue (11) to either side of a long straight stitched central shaft in dark orange to create the tail.

Moving On To The Bluebird . . .

5 On the bluebird follow the previous steps above to create the head, breast and neck: beak in grey; fine markings in black; head and throat in sky blue (12); upper breast in russet red. Blend russet red into dark orange under the wing covert (sky blue) and tick with white. Work the belly in white and soften the merged strata with fine shooting stitches in russet red. Work the feet in grey snake stitch overlaid with black as above.

6 Continue radial *opus plumarium* down the belly to the undertail coverts (grey).

Turning to the wing, work the central shaft of each feather in straight stitched grey. Following the colour chart, work narrow strata of directional *opus plumarium* on either side of each shaft in dull and sky blue.

On the tail, the central shafts of grey are surrounded by directional strata of grey-blue.

Complete each bird by careful reference to Plate 30 to make sure that every detail has been included – eye rings, highlights, leg details and so on.

7 In dark green (13) below and light green (14) above, work the segments of the bamboo canes in bands of very slightly angled directional work, following the curve of the design.

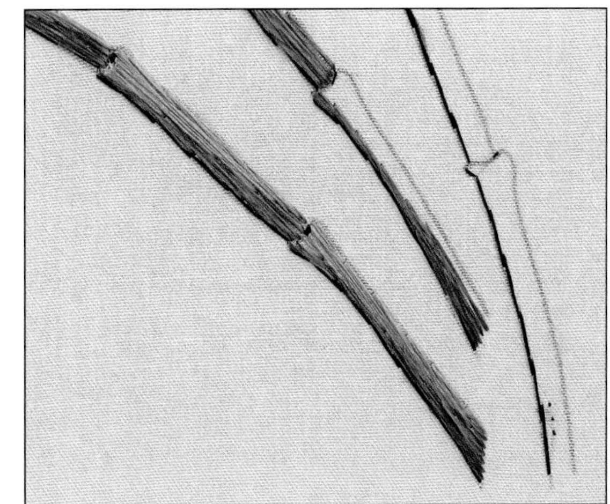

Finally, include whatever details you choose, grasses, water and so on, to make the picture your own. Remember that a cobweb (see Fig 22) should disappear *behind* any foreground features. Spiders are formed by just a few straight stitches to create a body and a few more to suggest the legs . . . easy!

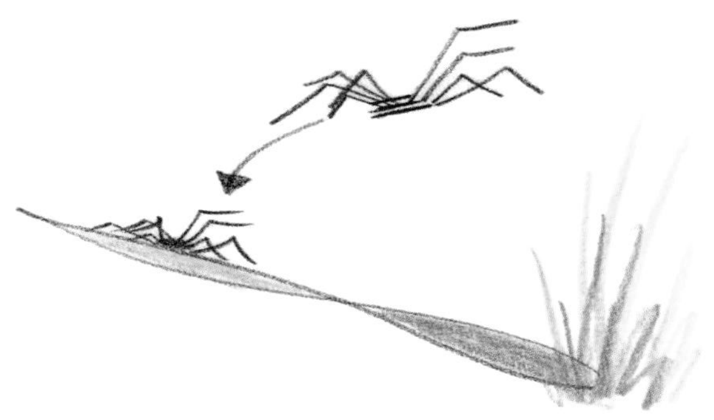

Materials

Fabric

The choice of fabric and threads can affect the ultimate appearance of any embroidery and, as with the choice of colourways, should be at the discretion of the embroiderer. However, to achieve satisfactory results, certain practical considerations need to be borne in mind.

For so-called flat-work embroidery which must be worked in a frame, it is essential that the fabric chosen for the background does not stretch. If the fabric stretches even slightly while the embroidery is in progress, when taken out of the frame it will contract to its normal size and the embroidery will be distorted. It is also a good idea to look for a smooth, evenweave fabric. Suitable fabrics include:

* Cotton
* Polyester cotton ('Percale')
* Linen

Pure silk may also be used, but avoid types with too much 'slub' in the weave as this will interrupt the flow of the embroidery stitches.

The embroideries in this book have been worked upon an inexpensive cotton/polyester fabric (sometimes called 'Percale') which is very lightweight. Poly-cotton mixes (evenweave) in a heavier weight are also ideal for use in this type of embroidery. Larger pictures should be worked on heavier fabrics, small studies on lightweights, but this rule can be adapted to the particular needs of the work in question.

When choosing fabric, try to avoid any fabrics which have too loose a weave, as this will result in too many stitches vying for space in too few threads of warp and weft. As a general rule, if the weave is open enough to be used for counted thread embroidery, it will be too wide for us!

◄ *Pure silks and cottons are available in a glorious variety of colours and textures. Clockwise from bottom left: stranded cottons, stranded and twisted silks, Japanese floss silk, fine floss silk, spun (fine twisted) silk.*

Threads

A variety of threads are necessary to achieve diverse effects but the ultimate choice of which type to use on any specific area is a personal one. Any thread suitable for 'flatwork' embroidery may be used for any of the techniques in this book. Natural fibres are easier to use than synthetics and include cotton,

* Cotton

Most embroiderers are familiar with stranded cotton. It is usually available in six-stranded skeins and strands should be used singly.

* Floss Silk

This is untwisted with a high sheen, and is also known as sleave or Japanese silk. It should be doubled or split (as appropriate to the type chosen) to match the gauge of a single strand of stranded cotton to complete most of the projects in this book.

* Twisted Silk

This usually has several strands twisted together. Single strands of most twisted silks are approximately the same gauge as single strands of stranded cotton and should be used singly. Very fine details should be worked in finer gauges of thread if available.

* Synthetic Metallic Threads

These are available in many formats in gold, silver and various other colours. The most versatile are several stranded threads which may be used entire where a thick gauge is required, or split into single strands for fine or delicate details.

❋ 'Real' Gold and Silver Thread
These threads are usually made using a percentage of real gold or silver. Generally they comprise very narrow strips of leaf or fine metal twisted around a synthetic, cotton or silk core. 'Passing' thread is tightly wound and available in various gauges, the finest of which may be used directly in the needle, the thicker couched down. 'Jap' gold is more loosely wound, is also available in a variety of gauges, but is usually only suitable for couching.

❋ Blending Filaments
This term encompasses a vast number of specialist threads, but usually refers to threads which are made up of a number of strands of differing types, e.g. a silky thread together with a cellophane or sparkling thread. They may be used entire, or split down into their component parts which may be used separately.

Tools

Basic embroidery tools have remained unchanged for centuries and the essentials are described here.

❋ Embroidery Frame
In flat embroidery the tension of the background fabric is all important (see Stitch Variations, page 92) and it is essential to work on an embroidery frame. Round, tambour hoops are best suited to fine embroidery as they produce an entirely uniform tension. Wooden hoops maintain their tension best. Always use a frame large enough to allow a generous amount of fabric around your design.

❋ Scissors
You will need small scissors for threads, fine and sharp. I use pinking shears for cutting fabric, which also helps to prevent fraying. Don't use thread or fabric scissors to cut anything else or you will blunt the blades.

❋ Needles
These should always be chosen with the specific use of threads and fabrics in mind. 'Embroidery' needles are designed with a long eye and a sharp point. A selection of sizes 5 to 10 are the most useful. Size 8 is ideal for use with a 'single strand' gauge as discussed above.

▼ *Floss and twisted silk produce different effects: glossy, as shown on the plant and upper sides of the butterflies' wings, or with the subtler, matt glow illustrated by the underside of the wings.*
10.75 x 12.75cm (4½ x 5in)

▲ *Metallic and specialist materials. Clockwise from top left: imitation gold thread (stranded), real gold passing thread, coloured metallic threads, real silver passing thread, blending filaments, imitation silver thread (stranded) with bugle and seed beads.*

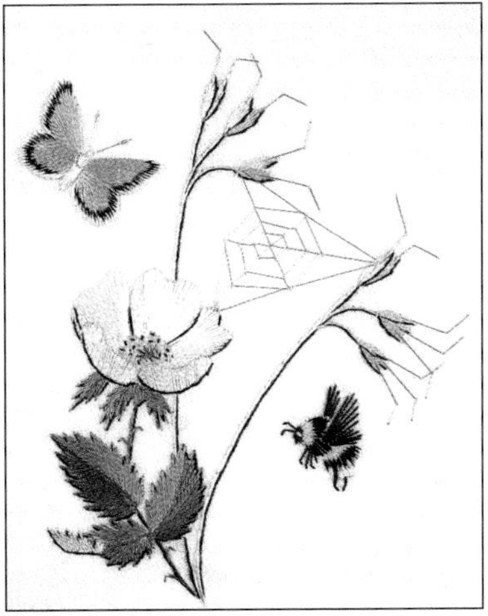

▲ *Working in stranded cotton and imitation metallic thread can create a soft, muted effect.*
10 x 12.75cm (4 x 5in)

Basic Techniques

Before you begin to embroider it is important to pay attention to the initial preparation and transfer of your design. Similarly, after your project is completed you need to give some thought to the presentation of the work.

Transferring a Design

You will need (see picture above, left to right):

- ❋ Original design
- ❋ Tracing paper (use good quality 90gsm)
- ❋ 'H' pencil
- ❋ Drawing pins
- ❋ Dressmakers' carbon paper in a colour contrasting your fabric
- ❋ Fabric
- ❋ Tissue paper
- ❋ Tambour hoop

You will also need scissors and a smooth, hard surface on which to work. Ideally, this should be a wooden drawing board covered with several layers of lining paper.

1 Place the tracing paper over your design and carefully trace off the design, omitting any very fine details, e.g., whiskers, spiders' webs, butterflies' antennae. These lines, if transferred, could not be covered by single strands of thread and must be added freehand during the course of the embroidery.

2 Lay your fabric flat, and place the tracing on top of it. Pin the tracing in place with two drawing pins at the top right and left-hand corners. Interleave between fabric and tracing

with the carbon (colour side down) and hold secure with a third pin through the tracing at the bottom of the paper. Do not pin through the carbon.

With a firm, even pressure, re-draw each line of the design. After you have completed a few lines, lift one corner of the tracing and carbon papers to check that the design is transferring successfully.

3 When the transfer is complete, remove the bottom drawing pin, lift back the tracing and remove the carbon paper. Check that every detail has been

transferred before finally removing the tracing paper. You are now ready to mount your fabric, using tissue paper and a tambour hoop (see instructions opposite).

Mounting Fabric in a Tambour Hoop

You will need:

- ✻ Fabric, with the design transferred
- ✻ Tissue paper
- ✻ Tambour hoop

1 Cut two sheets of tissue paper at least 5cm (2in) wider than the outer dimensions of your tambour hoop. Place the inner ring of your hoop on a flat surface and lay one sheet of tissue paper over it. Lay your fabric over the tissue paper, and ensure that the design is centred in the ring. Lay a second sheet of tissue paper over the fabric and slip the outer ring of the hoop over the entire 'sandwich'. Tighten the screw until the fabric and paper is held firmly.

2 Trim the upper sheet of tissue paper inside and outside the upper ring (shown above). Turn the hoop over and trim the lower sheet of tissue paper similarly. The tissue paper will protect your fabric from abrasion by the hoop and keep the handled edges clean. You are now ready to begin your embroidery.

Mounting and Framing Your Work

You will need (see picture above):

- ✻ Backing board (rigid cardboard, foamboard or hardboard)
- ✻ Acid free cartridge paper (cut to the same size as the backing board)
- ✻ Lacing thread (mercerised cotton is recommended)
- ✻ Two crewel needles (large enough to take the chosen cotton)
- ✻ Scissors

1 When your embroidery is complete press it on the wrong side, without steam (after checking the manufacturer's instructions for fabric and thread). Always press through another piece of fabric, and be *particularly* careful if you have used blending or other specialist filaments, especially cellophane threads.

It is essential to mount your work under similar tension to that exerted upon the fabric whilst in the tambour hoop. Lace it firmly onto a rigid backing board to achieve this tension. Make sure your backing board is large enough to take the whole design, with enough space at each edge to allow for framing.

2 Place the cartridge paper carefully between the board and the fabric. Next, position your embroidery, always making sure that the warp/left of the fabric lies straight in relation the edges of the board.

3 Invert the ensemble so that the embroidery is face down, with the cartridge paper and board on top of it. Cut the fabric to size, allowing a comfortable overlap. Fold the two sides in toward the centre of the board. Cut a long but manageable piece of lacing thread and thread a needle at each end, leaving two 'tails', of similar length.

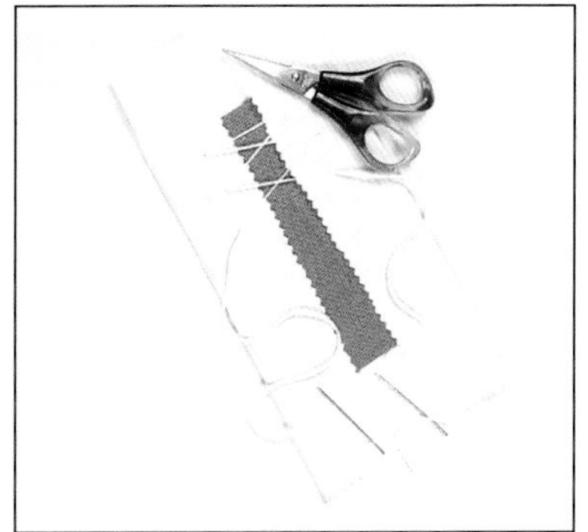

Working from the top, insert a needle on either side and lace the two sides of the fabric together, in corset fashion, until you reach the bottom. If you run out of thread simply tie the thread off and begin again.

4 Fold the top and bottom of the fabric toward the centre and repeat the lacing process. Always tie off the ends of the lacing thread with firm, non-slip knots and snip off any extra thread which is left. It takes a little practise to achieve the perfect tension. Do not over tighten the laces as the thread may break, or rip the fabric, but do not be afraid to exert a reasonable pull on the work as only in this way will the original tension of the fabric on the tambour hoop be re-created.

5 The choice of framing is a personal matter, but always be prepared to take professional advice as framing can make or mar a picture. A window mount is a good idea to keep the glass away from the fabric (essential if beads or thick specialist threads have been used) and remember that a frame should complement rather than dominate your design.

STITCH VARIATIONS

The stitches in this book are a combination of traditional embroidery stitches and contemporary innovations. They are flexible and adaptable: a single basic stitch such as stem stitch, depending on how it is applied, can produce a variety of effects, from a fine, sinuous line to a broad, strong one, with an infinite choice of widths, curves and reflexes within each variation.

The stitches fall into several distinct categories: linear, filling and decorative. Each has its own special properties and is suited to the description of certain shapes, fields and textures.

When working on a hoop the fabric *must* be taut within the frame. Stitches are always worked by the 'stab and pull' method. The needle is pushed through the fabric from above, the embroiderer's hand then moves to the back and pulls the needle through the fabric so the stitch forms smoothly on the surface. The next stitch is begun by pushing the needle up through the fabric from the reverse of the work, the hand brought to the front to pull the needle through, prior to beginning the routine once again.

LINEAR STITCHES

1 STEM STITCH

Always work from the top of any line to be described (on a natural history subject the outer extremity). Work *with* the curve of the subject: bring your needle out just to the outside of the curve and put it in on the inside of the curve.

a Fine/narrow stem stitch
Overlap the stitches by only a small proportion of the stitch length. The line created is only the width of a single stitch, creating a fine, sinuous effect.

b Broad stem stitch
Overlap the stitches so that half to three-quarters of each stitch lies beside its neighbour. The juxtaposition of several stitches creates a thick, strong effect.

c Graduating stem stitch
Begin with a fine stem stitch, increase it to a one-half ratio, then to three-quarters ratio within the same line creating the effect of a gradually thickening line (such as describes a growing stem – narrower at the tip, broader at the base).

d Coiling stem stitch
Begin with small stitches to describe the tight curve at the centre of the coil and gradually lengthen the stitches as the curve becomes gentler.

e Reflexing stem stitch
Beginning at the tip of the line, work the chosen variation a–c until the direction of the curve begins to change. Take one straight stitch through the preceding stitch, directly along the pattern line. Begin the stem stitch again, bringing the needle up on the new outside of the curve.

2 STRAIGHT STITCH

There are occasions when a completely straight line in the pattern can be described by a simple, straight stitch, or when a large field of the design must be filled smoothly with abutting straight stitches, such as in landscape work. The fabric must be taut within your frame to work this technique successfully.

a Vertical straight stitch (long)
Work this stitch from the top downward. Usually the stitches will be angled toward their base, such as in the case of simple grass effects. Ensure the stitch completely covers the transfer line.

b Horizontal straight stitch (long)
This stitch is used in blocks to suggest landscape effects. Work *toward* any abutting groups of stitches. To suggest a break in perspective, void (see 4 below) between abutting fields. To blend shades within a single field, stitch into the abutting field.

c Free straight stitch (long or short)
Fine details, such as whiskers, do not appear as transferred pattern lines (see Basic Techniques, page 90). These can be worked freehand in straight stitches angled to suit the particular needs of the subject matter. Work *away* from abutting groups of stitches.

3 SHADOW LINING

Establish the direction of the imagined light source within your picture. Each element of the design away from this light source will be shadow lined. Put a pin in the work, its tip pointing in the direction of the light source, to remind you of its origin.

a Smooth shadow lining
Work a fine, accurate stem stitch along the pattern line, just to its underside.

b Fragmented shadow lining
Where a line is too irregular to permit shadow lining by stem stitch, use straight stitches tailored to the length of the section of outline to be described.

4 VOIDING

Where two fields of a filling technique abut (see below), with or without a shadow line, suggesting that one element of the design overlaps another, a narrow line void of stitching should be left between the two. In practice, this forms on the transferred pattern line dividing the two elements. It should be approximately as wide as the gauge of thread used for the embroidery itself. To check that the width is correct, loosely position a strand of the thread along the 'valley' of the void. If it fits snugly, the width is correct.

FILLING STITCHES

1 OPUS PLUMARIUM

This literally means feather work and emulates the way in which feathers lie smoothly, yet with infinite changes of direction, upon a bird's body. The angle of the stitches sweeps around without breaking the flow of the stitching itself and this in turn catches the light, refracting it back from the stitching and giving a three-dimensional impression.

a Radial opus plumarium
(single or first stratum)
Begin with a stitch central to the field to be covered. This, and all subsequent stitches, are worked from the *outer* edge of the transferred pattern line *inwards* toward the centre of the motif. Bring the needle out immediately adjacent to the top of the first stitch. Slip the needle beneath the first stitch and through the fabric about two-thirds of the way down

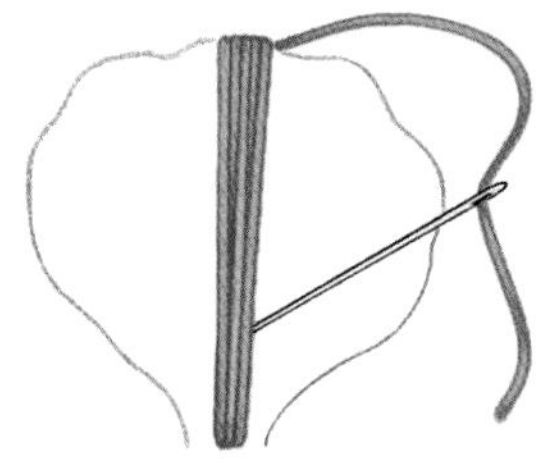

its length. This advances the angle of the stitching. Subsequent stitches can be either full length or shorter and angled as described, allowing the embroidery to fan out and cover the field without too many stitches 'bunching' at the inner core of the motif. A gradual advancement of the angle is achieved by working the angled stitches longer (e.g., three-quarters of the length of full stitches), more acute advancement of the angle by working them shorter (one quarter to half of the length of the full stitches).

b Radial opus plumarium
(subsequent strata)
Where a broad field of stitches is

required to fill a motif, several strata of *opus plumarium* may be required.

Work the first stratum by the single stratum method described above. Always stitching *inwards* (toward the core of the motif), work the second stratum by taking a first stitch at the centre of the field. Stitch into the first stratum (do not leave a void) and, following the established flow of the stitching, fan out on either side of the first stitch, advancing the angle when necessary, as before. Subsequent strata are worked similarly.

c Directional opus plumarium
(single or first stratum)
Where the core of the motif is elongated (such as the central vein of a simple elliptic leaf) the stitches should flow smoothly along its length. Again, always stitch inwards, bringing the needle out

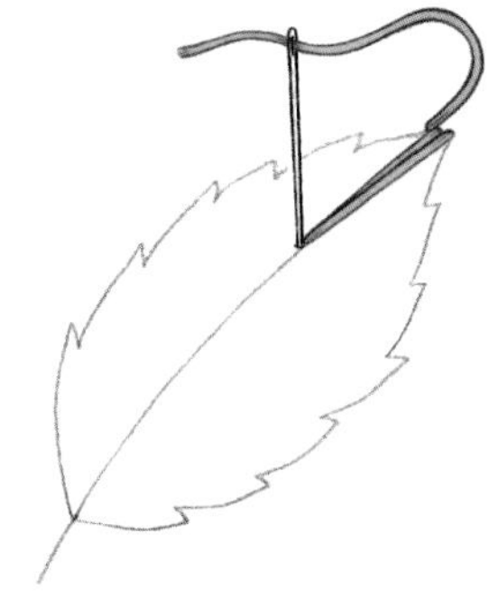

at the outer edge of the motif and in toward its centre.

Begin at the tip of the motif (or outer extremity of the first stratum) and take the first stitch inwards to abut the tip of the elongated core. Work your way down the field to be covered advancing the angle as necessary, as described above (a).

d Directional opus plumarium
(subsequent strata)
Work the first strata as described above. Again working from the direction of the

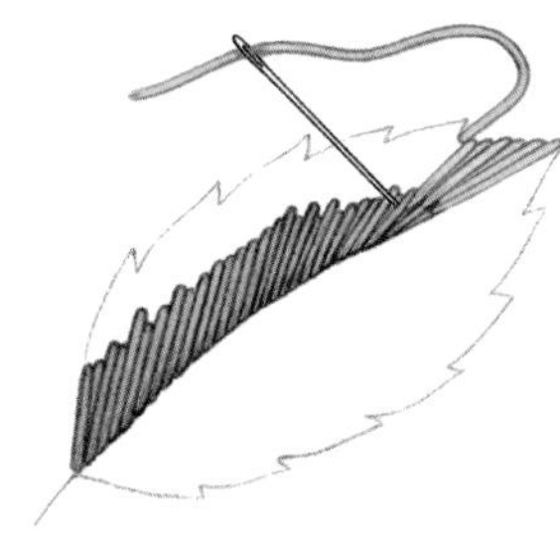

tip of the motif inwards, create subsequent strata by stitching into the previous stratum (do not void), advancing the angle of the stitching as necessary to match the abutting stitches.

2 Opposite Angle Stitching

This is used to create the effect of reflex, e.g., where a leaf or petal curls forward or backward to reveal its underside.

Following the principles of *opus plumarium* work the stitches at an exactly opposite angle to the abutting field. (Occasionally the angles will be similar in actuality, but opposite in relation to the concept of the directional stitching.) Where necessary void between the two.

3 Snake Stitch

This is used to describe long, sinuous shapes, such as broad blades of grass or other linear leaves.

a Simple snake stitch
Begin at the tip of the motif, taking the first stitch in the direction of the curve to be described. For subsequent stitches, bring the needle out on the *outside* of

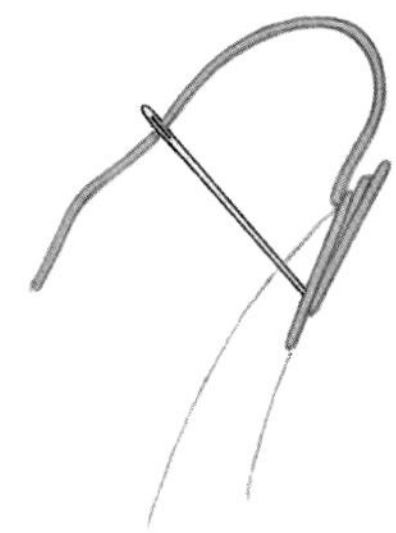

the curve and in on the *inside*. Work smoothly down the motif, advancing the angle of stitches, if necessary, by the *opus plumarium* method and lengthening the stitches where appropriate, as with graduating stem stitch (see above).

b Reflexing snake stitch
Begin at the point of reflex, where the direction of the curve changes. Firstly, take a stitch angled across the field slanting between the tip and base of the

curve. Work upwards to the tip, bringing the needle out on the outside of the curve and in on the inside until the upper field is complete. Advance the angle of stitching by the *opus plumarium* method if necessary. Complete the lower field by returning to the central stitch and working down the motif, again bringing the needle out on the outside and in on the inside of the curve. Advance the stitch angle as necessary.

4 Dalmatian Dog Technique

This is used to create a single, smooth field of embroidery where an area of one colour is completely encompassed by another colour. Used within *opus plumarium* (either radial or directional).

a Simple Dalmatian dog

Establish the radial or directional flow of the *opus plumarium*. Working the stitches at exactly the same angle as the main field of *opus plumarium* to follow,

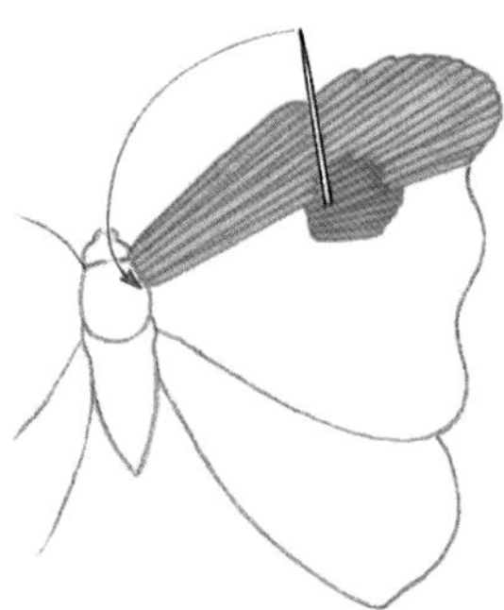

work the spots or other fields to be covered first. When completed, flood the rest of the *opus plumarium* around them, again paying careful attention to the flow of the stitches.

b Multiple Dalmatian dog

This technique can create a 'spot within a spot' or any other irregular pattern.

Establish either the radial or directional flow of the *opus plumarium*.

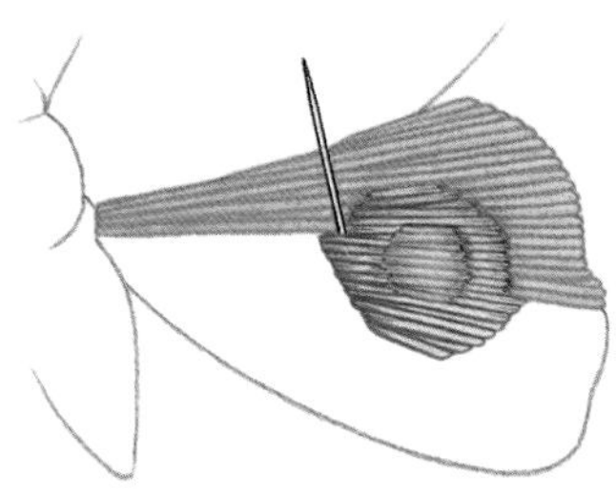

Maintaining the angle of stitching as above, work the innermost colour first, followed by outer field or fields of colour until the spots or other shapes are complete. Flood the surrounding *opus plumarium* around them.

Decorative Stitches

1 Seed Stitch

Fine, short, straight stitches worked directly onto the fabric, occasionally superimposed over other embroidery.

2 Ticking

These are seed stitches overlaying *opus plumarium*, worked at exactly the same angle as the underlying work but taken in the opposite direction, i.e., against the flow of the work.

3 Studding

These are seed stitches which overlay *opus plumarium*, but are worked at right angles to the underlying stitches.

4 Shooting Stitch

Long straight stitches taken in the opposite direction to the underlying radial or directional work.

5 Chevron Stitch

Two long straight stitches are angled to meet. Infill with a third straight stitch if necessary. To create a very sharp angle (such as a thistle spike) work a fourth straight stitch in a fine gauge of thread through the body of the motif.

6 Dotting/Speckling

Work very short straight stitches, only as long as the width of the thread, to create an impression of tiny round dots. Work the stitches close together and in random directions.

7 Floating Embroidery

This allows the threads to lie loosely on the fabric, falling into spontaneous shapes. Do not transfer the design to be formed onto the background fabric.

Take a long stitch from the inside to the outside of the motif, putting a finger or pencil under the thread to keep it away from the fabric. Take a very small stitch at the outer point of the motif to bring the thread back to the

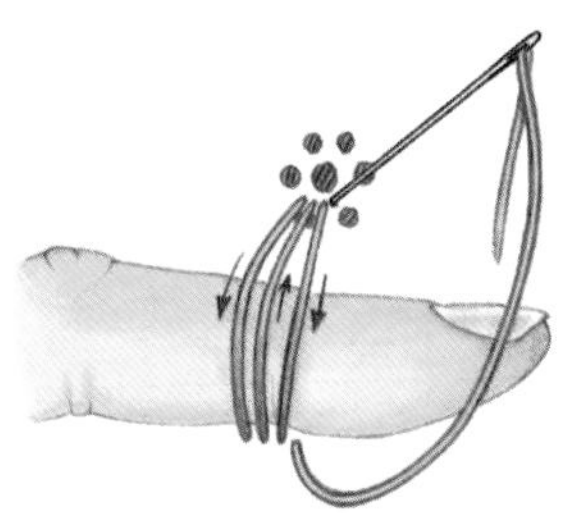

surface. Take a third stitch back to the core of the motif, again keeping a finger beneath the thread. Repeat the process, removing the finger or pencil when several strands have built up.

8 Surface Couching

Usually a goldwork technique, this can be used effectively on various threads.

Bring the thread to be couched (the base thread) through the fabric to the surface of the work. If it is too thick to be brought through the fabric, lay it in place and hold it down with a thumb. Thread a second needle with a finer thread (the couching thread) and bring it up through the fabric immediately alongside the base thread. Take a tiny stitch over the base thread, at right angles to it, and repeat at regular intervals, effectively using the couching thread to whip the base thread into place along the transferred pattern line. Pay particular attention to whipping the beginning and the end of the base thread into place if it is lying wholly on the surface of the work.

9 Subdued Voiding

Where two fields of *opus plumarium* abut and are separated by a voided line, the effect can be softened by working fine straight stitches, at the angle of the underlying work, across the void. Use a shade similar to that of the embroidered field 'closer' in perspective to the viewer, e.g., where a bird's wing lies over its body, or the angle of its neck creates a break in perspective. Work the overlying stitches at regular intervals, allowing the voided line to show through.

Suppliers

There are many manufacturers and suppliers of embroidery materials and equipment and I have suggested a few here.
** This indicates suppliers who will accept orders direct from the given address via mail order.*

Coats Crafts UK,
PO Box 22, The Lingfield Estate,
McMullen Road, Darlington,
Co. Durham DL1 1YQ, UK
Tel: 01325 365457
Stranded cottons

Coats and Clark,
Susan Bates Inc.,
30 Patewood Drive,
Greenville, SC 29615, USA
Tel: (US) 800 241 5997
Stranded cottons

DMC Creative World Ltd.,
Pullman Road, Wigston,
Leicestershire LE18 2DY, UK
Tel: 0116 281 1040
Fax: 0116 281 3592
Website: www.dmc/cw.com
Stranded cotton, imitation gold and silver thread

DMC Corporation,
Building 10, Port Kearny,
South Kearny, NJ 07032, USA
Tel: (US) 201 589 0606
Stranded cotton, imitation gold and silver thread

Japanese Embroidery Centre UK,*
White Lodge, Littlewick Road,
Lower Knaphill, Woking,
Surrey GU21 2JU, UK
Tel: 01483 476246
Floss silk, real gold and silver threads, imitation gold, silver and coloured metallic threads

Kreinik Manufacturing. Co., Inc.,
3106 Timanus Lane, Suite 101,
Baltimore, MD 21244, USA
Tel: (US) 800 537 2166
(UK ++01325 365 457)
Website: http://www.kreinik.com
E-mail: kreinik@kreinik.com
Blending filaments and metallic threads

Madeira Threads (UK) Ltd.,
PO Box 6, Thirsk,
North Yorkshire YO7 3BX, UK
Tel: 01845 524880
E-mail: acts@madeira
Website: www.madeira.co.uk
Twisted/stranded silks

Pearsall's,
Tancrad Street, Taunton,
Somerset TA1 1RY, UK
Tel: 01823 274700
Shop online at
www.pearsallsembroidery.com
Stranded pure silk thread

Pipers Specialist Silks, *
Chinnerys, Egremont Street,
Glemsford, Sudbury,
Suffolk CI10 7SA, UK
Tel: 01787 280920
Website: http://www.pipers-silks.com
E-mail: susanpeck@pipers-silks.com
Floss and spun (twisted) silk. Exclusive silk kits designed by Helen M. Stevens

Stephen Simpson Ltd., *
50 Manchester Road,
Preston PR1 3YH, UK
Tel: 01772 556688
Real gold and silver threads

The Voirrey Embroidery Centre, *
Brimstage Hall,
Wirral L63 6JA, UK
Tel: 0151 3423514
General embroidery supplies

Helen M. Stevens
(Enquiries via David & Charles or website below)
Website: www.helenmstevens.co.uk
For embroidery masterclass tutorials, lectures and commissions

Acknowledgements

I am grateful to my clients for the inclusion of certain Plate numbers: 19, Elizabeth Hudd; 17 and 23, Luizella Strona; 24, Denise Whalley; 29, Jean and Brian Smith. Thanks also to Nigel Salmon for his wonderful photography, to David and Charles and to friends and family who encouraged the project throughout.

INDEX

BIRDS AND COMPANION FLORA AND FAUNA

Italic page numbers indicate plates; **bold** page numbers indicate figures.

STITCHES AND TECHNIQUES